THE COSMOLOGICAL
ARGUMENT

THE COSMOLOGICAL
∾ARGUMENT∾

William L. Rowe

PRINCETON UNIVERSITY PRESS

Library of Congress Cataloging in Publication data will
be found on the last printed page of this book

Publication of this book has been aided by
The Andrew W. Mellon Foundation

This book has been composed in Linotype Baskerville

Printed in the United States of America
by Princeton University Press, Princeton, New Jersey

For My Parents

Acknowledgments

THE editors of *Man and World* have kindly given me permission for the use of parts of my article "The Cosmological Argument and the Principle of Sufficient Reason," published in 1968 (2, pp. 278-292); the editor of *The Monist* has permitted me to incorporate in Chapter III part of my article "Two Criticisms of the Cosmological Argument," published 1970 (Vol. 54, no. 3); and Wayne State University Press has granted me permission for the use of parts of my article "The Cosmological Argument," published in *Nous*, February 1971. Among those who have provided me with useful suggestions and helpful criticisms concerning some of the central ideas in this study, I want to explicitly thank: Marilyn Adams, Bob Adams, Bill Forgie, Bill Gustason, Father Joseph Owens, Alvin Plantinga, John Stevens, Ted Ulrich, Henry Veatch, and Bill Wainwright. To Frank Parker I owe a special debt of gratitude for advice concerning the manuscript and encouragement while I was engaged in writing it. Also, I want to thank the reader for Princeton University Press for many helpful suggestions and criticisms.

Contents

THE COSMOLOGICAL
ARGUMENT

Introduction

ARGUMENTS for the existence of God are commonly divided into *a posteriori* arguments and *a priori* arguments. An *a posteriori* argument depends on a principle or premise that can be known only by means of our experience of the world. The premise or principle in question may assert nothing more than that certain things exist that have been caused to exist by other things. Or it may assert something as complicated as that the world contains a large number of things whose parts are so arranged that, under proper conditions, they work together to achieve a certain end. An *a priori* argument, on the other hand, purports to rest on principles all of which can be known independently of our experience of the world, by just reflecting on and understanding them. Of the three major theistic arguments—the Cosmological, Teleological, and Ontological—only the last is an *a priori* argument; the Cosmological Argument and the Teleological Argument are *a posteriori* arguments.

Although the above division is correct as far as it goes, it will mislead us if we conclude that the really basic principles appealed to in the Cosmological Argument are *a posteriori*. The proponents of the Cosmological Argument insist that the fundamental principles appealed to in the argument are necessary truths, known either directly or by deduction from other *a priori* principles that are known directly. To a lesser extent, this is true of the Teleological Argument as well. The arguments are *a posteriori* in that they begin by reasoning

3

about facts concerning our world that we know by means of experience. The principles appealed to in reasoning about these facts, however, are principles that the proponents of the arguments would call *a priori* truths. Such a principle, as we shall see, is the Principle of Sufficient Reason, the pivot on which the Cosmological Argument turns.

Among the differences between the two *a posteriori* arguments, the Cosmological and the Teleological, three are worth noting. First, the fact about the world from which the Teleological Argument begins is vastly more complicated and, therefore, more difficult to establish by experience than is the fact from which the Cosmological Argument proceeds. The Cosmological Argument generally concerns itself with some simple fact such as that there are things that are being changed by other things, or that there are things that owe their existence to other things. The Teleological Argument, however, begins by claiming that the world itself is like a machine or, at least, that many things in the world such as animals, plants, etc., are machine-like in that their parts are so ordered as to work together to serve a certain end. Second, the Teleological Argument is an inductive argument; its premises, if true, may lend considerable support to its conclusion, but do not demonstrate or establish its truth. The Cosmological Argument, on the other hand, is a deductive argument; its premises, if true, may establish the truth of its conclusion. Finally, the Teleological Argument does not purport to be a complete argument for the existence of the theistic God. At best it may render it probable that the cause of the world has a high degree of intelligence and power. But that the cause of the world is *infinitely* powerful and intelligent, all-knowing, all-good, etc., lies be-

yond the scope of the Teleological Argument to establish or even render highly probable. The Cosmological
Argument, however, like the Ontological Argument,
purports to be a complete argument for the existence
of the theistic God; it purports to establish the existence
of a being and its possession of the attributes—omnip-
otence, omniscience, goodness, etc.—commonly associated with the theistic concept of God.

The Cosmological Argument, as it shall be understood in this study, has two quite distinct parts. The
first part is an argument to establish the existence of a
first mover, first efficient cause, a necessary being, or,
more generally, a being that accounts for the existence
of the world. It is popular to identify the Cosmological
Argument with what, according to this study, is only its
first part. Thus, for example, Aquinas's argument for a
first efficient cause (the second way) is often spoken of as
a version of "the Cosmological Argument." The major
reason for not identifying the Cosmological Argument
with what I have called its "first part" is that, if we do
so identify it, we must conclude either that the argument does not purport to establish the existence of the
theistic God or that, if it does, it completely fails to do
so. Since the Cosmological Argument is generally understood to be an argument for the existence of the theistic
God, the first alternative may be rejected. The second
alternative, however, judges the argument a failure
from the outset. For if the argument purports to establish the existence of the theistic God when in fact it, at
best, establishes the existence of a first efficient cause
or a necessary being, then the argument is obviously a
failure. We can always ask the skeptical question: "Why
must a first efficient cause or a necessary being have the
properties of the theistic God?" And, of course, the

Cosmological Argument, if identified with its first part, will not provide us with an answer to this question. The Cosmological Argument, therefore, as understood in this study, consists of two parts. The first part, depending on which version we pursue, is an argument to establish the existence of a first cause, necessary being, or a being that accounts for the existence of the world. The second part is an argument to establish that the being established in the first part is God, that is, has the properties associated with the theistic concept of God. A good deal of philosophical criticism has been directed against the first part of the argument. Much less has been directed against the second part of the argument. In this study I shall be concerned mainly with the first part of the argument. In the interest of completeness, however, some attention will be given to the issues involved in the second part of the argument.

The Cosmological Argument began with Plato and Aristotle, flourished in the writings of Aquinas and Duns Scotus in the thirteenth century, was forcefully presented in the eighteenth century by Leibniz and Samuel Clarke, and has been severely criticized in the modern period by philosophers of the stature of Hume, Kant, and Bertrand Russell. Although I shall argue that the major criticisms of the Cosmological Argument either rest on philosophical mistakes or fail to refute the argument, my principal aim throughout this study is neither to refute the criticisms nor to defend the argument. My main purpose is to uncover, clarify, and critically examine the philosophical concepts and theses essential to the reasoning exhibited in the Cosmological Argument.

There are a number of versions or forms of the Cosmological Argument. Apart from the versions in Plato and Aristotle, which represent the early beginnings of the argument, the most forceful and, historically, the most significant versions of the argument appeared in the writing of Aquinas and Duns Scotus in the thirteenth century and in the writings of Leibniz and Samuel Clarke in the eighteenth century. There are, of course, other versions of the Cosmological Argument. These additional versions may be divided into two classes. The first class consists of further historical specimens of the argument—for example, Descartes' version in the third Meditation—that are of less significance than those mentioned above. The second class consists of contemporary statements of the argument by philosophers intent either on explicating earlier versions or on developing an improved version of the argument.[1]

From the above, it should be clear that no single argument can lay claim to being *the* Cosmological Argument. The Cosmological Argument represents a family of arguments, arguments that generally start from some relatively simple fact about the world and, by appealing to the Principle of Sufficient Reason or some principle governing causality, endeavor to establish the existence of a being that has the properties of the theistic

[1] Wallace Matson, for example, in *The Existence of God* (Ithaca: Cornell University Press, 1965) presents a version of the argument which "in its main outlines," he contends, follows Leibniz's version (p. 61). But Matson's version, if good, establishes the existence of a necessary being only in the sense of a being that cannot be caused by anything else. It does not establish the existence of a necessary being in the sense of a being whose non-existence is logically impossible. Leibniz's version of the argument is designed to yield the conclusion that there exists a being whose non-existence is logically impossible. Hence, what Matson has done is present a version of the Cosmological Argument that is substantially different from the Leibniz-Clarke argument.

7

God. Within this family are a variety of arguments, some quite crude, others highly sophisticated. My own belief is that the most sophisticated and fully developed form of the argument is the eighteenth-century version developed by Samuel Clarke in the first series of his Boyle lectures delivered in 1704. These lectures, published under the title *A Demonstration of the Being and Attributes of God*, constitute, I believe, the most complete, forceful, and cogent presentation of the Cosmological Argument we possess.[2] It was of the arguments presented in these lectures that the logician George Boole remarked: ". . . they are almost always specimens of correct logic, and they exhibit a subtlety of apprehension and a force of reasoning which have seldom been equalled, never perhaps surpassed."[3]

In this study we shall examine the historically significant versions of the Cosmological Argument that appeared in the thirteenth century and the sophisticated version that appeared in the writings of Clarke and Leibniz in the eighteenth century. As we shall see, these versions differ considerably from one another. Criticisms that may be definitive against one version of the argument may turn out to be utterly irrelevant to some

[2] The second series of lectures—delivered in 1705—was published under the title, *A Discourse Concerning the Unchangeable Obligations of Natural Religion and the Truth and Certainty of the Christian Revelation*. The two series were subsequently published together in one volume with the title, *A Discourse Concerning the Being and Attributes of God, The Obligations of Natural Religion, and the Truth and Certainty of the Christian Revelation*. References are to the ninth edition of this work, printed by W. Botham for John and Paul Knapton, London, 1738. Hereafter references to the *Demonstration* will appear in the text.

[3] George Boole, *The Laws of Thought*, first published in 1854, reprinted by Dover (New York), p. 187.

other important version. On the other hand, we shall see that all versions of the argument rely on some form of the Principle of Sufficient Reason. We shall begin with a study of the thirteenth-century forms of the Cosmological Argument and proceed to an analysis and evaluation of the argument as developed by Samuel Clarke in the eighteenth century.

I

The Cosmological Argument in
Aquinas and Duns Scotus

T HE first three of Aquinas's "Five Ways" constitute three distinct, important versions of the
Cosmological Argument.[1] If we use the translation of the Blackfriars edition, the first way proceeds
as follows:

> The first and most obvious way is based on change.
> Some things in the world are certainly in process of
> change: this we plainly see. Now anything in process
> of change is being changed by something else. This is
> so because it is characteristic of things in process of
> change that they do not yet have the perfection towards
> which they move, though able to have it; whereas it is
> characteristic of something causing change to have that
> perfection already. For to cause change is to bring into
> being what was previously only able to be, and this can
> only be done by something that already is: thus fire,
> which is actually hot, causes wood, which is able to be
> hot, to become actually hot, and in this way causes
> change in the wood. Now the same thing cannot at the
> same time be both actually X and potentially X,
> though it can be actually X and potentially Y: the
> actually hot cannot at the same time be potentially
> hot, though it can be potentially cold. Consequently, a
> thing in process of change cannot itself cause that same

[1] The first two ways share a common style of reasoning. The
third, as we shall see, differs considerably from the first two ways.

change; it cannot change itself. Of necessity therefore anything in process of change is being changed by something else. Moreover, this something else, if in process of change, is itself being changed by yet another thing; and this last by another. Now we must stop somewhere, otherwise there will be no first cause of the change, and, as a result, no subsequent causes. For it is only when acted upon by the first cause that the intermediate causes will produce the change: if the hand does not move the stick, the stick will not move anything else. Hence one is bound to arrive at some first cause of change not itself being changed by anything, and this is what everybody understands by God.[2]

Before examining the structure of this argument, we need to note that this is only the first part of the Cosmological Argument: that is, an argument to establish the existence of an unchanged changer, a first cause of change, which itself is not in a process of change. After concluding his argument for the unchanged changer, Aquinas simply adds "and this is what everybody understands by God." But, of course, there is a serious question as to whether an unchanged changer need have the properties of the theistic God. It would be unfair to Aquinas, however, to charge him with simply assuming that an unchanged changer would have to be God. For in other sections of the *Summa Theologica*, Aquinas presents rational arguments designed to demonstrate that the unchanged changer must possess the properties associated with the theistic concept of God.[3]

[2] *Summa Theologica*, 1a. 2, 3. Hereafter, references to this work will be abbreviated as ST.

[3] See Father Copleston's remark on this issue in *A History of Philosophy*, Vol. II (Westminster: The Newman Press, 1960), pp. 342-343.

The argument to establish the existence of an un-changed changer represents, therefore, a major version of the *first part* of the Cosmological Argument. The complete development of the Cosmological Argument in Aquinas's *Summa Theologica* extends far beyond his brief statement of the first three ways.

By "change" Aquinas means to include change in place, change in quantity (for example, something be-coming larger or smaller), and change in quality (for example, something changing from being cold to being hot). The argument, I believe, is more forceful when the change in question is of the third sort, change in quality; but in appraising the argument I shall not limit the discussion to examples of qualitative change.

The argument begins with a fact about the world that experience teaches us—namely, some things change.

    1. Some things are in a process of change.

The next premise in the argument represents what Aquinas would view as a metaphysical principle estab-lished by *a priori* reasoning, rather than a fact estab-lished by experience.

    2. Whatever is in a process of change is being changed by something else.

Aquinas recognizes the need to establish this premise and, therefore, tries to support it by an argument. We shall examine his argument for (2) below.

    3. An infinite regress of changers, each changed by another is impossible.

(3) has often been denied by critics of the argument. We shall examine (3) and Aquinas's argument for it.

Therefore:

4. *There is a first cause of change, itself not in a process of change.*

The core of this argument, as Aquinas clearly recognized, consists of the two claims: that whatever is changing is being changed by something else, and that an infinite regress of changers, each changed by another, is impossible. Let us begin our analysis of the argument by examining Aquinas's argument in support of premise (2).

If something is in a process of qualitative change then, on Aquinas's view, it is coming to be in a certain state that it is not now actually in. For example, if the water in the kettle is changing from being cold to being boiling hot, then it can be said to be coming to be in the state of being boiling hot, but just so long as it is *coming to be* in that state, it is not yet in that state, but in a state somewhere between cold and boiling hot. Now if something is not actually in a certain state but can come to be in that state—as water that is not actually hot nevertheless can become hot—it is, in Aquinas's view, *potentially* in that state, but not *actually* in it Thus cold water is potentially hot but not actually hot, and hot water is potentially cold, but not actually cold. These considerations lead Aquinas to the principle that nothing can be both actually and potentially in the same state at the same time. "Now the same thing cannot at the same time be both actually X and potentially X, though it can be actually X and potentially Y: the actually hot cannot at the same time be potentially hot, though it can be potentially cold." So far Aquinas's reasoning seems cogent, but we are still a major step away from establishing that whatever is in a process of change is being changed by something else.

We come now to the crucial step in Aquinas's argument for premise (2). Aquinas claims that if something is in a process of change toward a state A, there must be something *actually in state A* that is causing the thing in question to be changing toward state A. This is the most plausible interpretation of his remark: "For to cause change is to bring into being what was previously only able to be, and this can only be done by something that already is: thus fire, which is actually hot, causes wood, which is able to be hot, to become actually hot, and in this way causes change in the wood."

There are two major objections to this fundamental claim in Aquinas's reasoning in support of premise (2). But before considering these objections, we need to see the basic role Aquinas's claim plays in his argument for premise (2). That argument may be exhibited as follows:

    i. If something is in a process of change toward a state A, then it is potentially in state A.

    ii. If something is in a process of change toward state A, there must be something which is actually in state A which is causing the thing in question to be changing toward state A.

    iii. Nothing can be both actually in state A and potentially in state A at the same time.

Therefore:

    2. *Whatever is in a process of change is being changed by something else.*

As I noted above, there are two major objections to the crucial step (ii) in Aquinas's argument for (2). First, it does not seem to be universally true that if one thing causes a second thing to change toward a certain state, the first thing must actually be in that state. It does seem true that if something makes water become hot, it must itself be hot. But suppose a plant is in a process of dying. Must that which causes the plant to be changing toward the state of being dead be something that itself is already actually dead? Moreover, doesn't Aquinas believe that God can directly cause cold water to become hot? But it makes no sense to say that God is in the state of being hot. Perhaps Aquinas only meant to assert that if one thing causes a second thing to be changing toward a certain state, the first thing must actually be in that state or have all that that state represents in another form. Thus, although God is not actually hot, He has all the power that is represented by the state of heat. However, once we begin to qualify Aquinas's basic principle in this way, the principle becomes vague to a degree that renders it difficult to understand exactly what is being asserted and it becomes less clear that a thing cannot cause a change to take place in itself. Thus, according to the first objection, if we take Aquinas's principle literally there seem to be counter-examples to it. On the other hand, if we try to qualify the principle by not insisting that the cause *actually* be in the state it is causing another to change toward, the principle becomes vague and difficult to understand with the result that it becomes less than certain that a thing cannot cause itself to change toward a certain state. For while it is clear that nothing can be both actually and potentially in a given state at the same time, it is not so clear that a thing might have the power or degree of reality represented by a certain state even though it is not actually in that state.

It is not difficult to see the fundamental idea underlying Aquinas's reasoning. If something undergoes a change and, as a result, comes to have some feature it did not previously possess, it would seem that the only way it could get this feature is from something that already has it. Since it itself did not have it, it cannot have been the cause of the change it underwent in coming to acquire it. Nor could anything else that lacked that feature have caused this thing to come to acquire that feature. To suppose otherwise would be to suppose that something comes from nothing. Consequently, whatever causes a thing to come to possess something must be a thing that already has that something and, hence, can impart it to the thing that is undergoing a change.

As attractive as this fundamental idea seems to be, it conceals an assumption of enormous importance, and it is the point of the second major objection to bring this assumption to the surface. We can get at this assumption best by noting that Aquinas considers only two alternatives in discussing the fact that some things are in a process of change. He considers the possibility that a thing might be the cause of its own process of change, and he considers the possibility that something else might be the cause of the change that a thing is undergoing. What he does not consider is a third possibility: namely, that it is simply a brute fact that certain things are changing. Of course, we know that many things which are changing are being changed by other things—thus the water is being changed from cold to hot by something else, the fire. But the question is: Why may not there be some things in a process of change that are neither causing themselves to change nor being changed by other things? Suppose we say that it is a *brute fact* that X is changing just in case X is changing but there is no thing that is causing it to change. And the question is: What reasons does Aquinas give for ruling out the possibility that it is a brute fact that certain things are changing? The answer is that Aquinas gives no reasons for ruling out this possibility. He simply does not consider it a genuine possibility. Thus after ruling out the possibility that a thing causes itself to change, Aquinas immediately infers: "Of necessity therefore anything in process of change is being changed by something else." Underlying this inference is a basic assumption, namely, *that it is never a brute fact that something is changing*.

The second major objection calls this assumption into question. Why should we believe that it is never a brute fact that something is changing? Of course, if there were such a brute fact, then there would be some fact that is without any causal explanation. And if a causal explanation is the only form of explanation appropriate when the fact in question is some thing changing from one state to another, then to admit brute facts is to admit facts that are unintelligible in the sense that they admit of no explanation. But again: Why not admit that some facts involving change are ultimate in the sense that, while they may enter into an explanation of other facts, they themselves have no explanation whatever? Having raised this question in the form of an objection to Aquinas's reasoning for premise (2), we need pursue it no further for the moment. Questions like it will be considered in some detail later in this study. For the moment it is sufficient to note that Aquinas is assuming for purposes of his argument that there are no brute facts involving qualitative change. The point of the objection is simply to bring this assumption to the surface and to question its truth.

Thus far Aquinas has argued that some things are in a process of change and whatever is in a process of change is being changed by something else. Now if we start with something that is in a process of change, we must, in tracing the causes of its process of change, be faced either with an infinite regress of changers, each in a process of change and therefore being changed by something else, or the regress must terminate somewhere in a cause of change that itself is unchanging. The final step in Aquinas's argument is to establish that:

3. *An infinite regress of changers, each changed by another is impossible.* Its got to end.

His argument is that if there is no first cause of change, itself unchanging, there cannot be anything in a process of change. "For it is only when acted upon by the first cause that the intermediate causes will produce the change: if the hand does not move the stick, the stick will not move anything else." On the surface, it must be admitted that Aquinas's argument appears to be nothing more than a rather crude instance of question-begging. We want to know why Aquinas thinks the series must terminate in a first changer, itself unchanging, rather than regressing to infinity, each cause of change itself in a process of change and, therefore, being changed by something else. In response to our inquiry, Aquinas in effect says nothing more than that, in a series *which has a first member*, if that first member does not cause change then there will be no process of change in any member of the series. And this seems true

18

enough. But, of course, our question was not why *in a series with a first member* the first member must be causing change in order for other members in the series to be in a process of change, but why need there be a first member in a series in which there are members in a process of change. In giving the answer he does, Aquinas appears to *assume* that every series in which there are members in a process of change *has a first member*. But this is precisely the issue he has undertaken to establish. Hence, his argument begs the very question at issue.

When a philosopher of the stature of Aquinas offers an argument that appears to be a textbook example of a question-begging argument, it is sometimes wise to search for something beneath the surface that may have been poorly expressed but, nevertheless, may represent his real view on the subject. Although, as stated, Aquinas's argument is, I believe, question-begging, perhaps there is more to his view than meets the eye. In any case, at the risk of misinterpreting Aquinas, I shall suggest a line of reasoning against the infinite regress that may represent at least part of his view on the subject. However, since Aquinas again argues against the infinite regress in the second way and since the interpretation I wish to suggest is more easily presented in connection with the second way, I shall postpone its development for the moment.

In the second way, Aquinas again argues from causation. But here it is the cause of a thing's existence and not of a process of change taking place within an existing thing that is the initial focus of his attention.

The second way is based on the nature of causation. In the observable world causes are found to be ordered in series; we never observe, nor ever could, something causing itself, for this would mean it preceded itself, and this is not possible. Such a series of causes must however stop somewhere; for in it an earlier member causes an intermediate and the intermediate a last (whether the intermediate be one or many). Now if you eliminate a cause you also eliminate its effects, so that you cannot have a last cause, nor an intermediate one, unless you have a first. Given therefore no stop in the series of causes, and hence no first cause, there would be no intermediate causes either, and no last effect, and this would be an open mistake. One is therefore forced to suppose some first cause, to which everyone gives the name "God."[4]

Perhaps the first point that comes to mind—or, more accurately, strikes the eye—when the second way is compared with the first is that the second way is a much shorter argument. The reason for this is clear. In each way there are two points to be established. First, that no thing can be its own cause; second, that an infinite regress of causes is impossible. Now in the second way, the first point is obvious. For in the second way, it is the existence of a thing we are initially inquiring about, and it seems obvious that no thing can be the cause of its own existence. Thus in the second way the first point to be established is so obvious as not to require much in the way of argument. In the first way, however, it is not a thing's existence that is the initial object of inquiry, but the fact that an existing thing is in a process of change toward some state, and it is far from obvious that some thing cannot cause itself to undergo a change. Hence, Aquinas feels compelled to present a fairly elab-

[4] ST, 1a. 2, 3.

orate argument to establish the first point in the first way, and this accounts for the fact that the first way is double the length of the second.

Aquinas's second way may be stated as follows:

1. *Some things exist and their existence is caused.*
2. *Whatever is caused to exist is caused to exist by something else.*
3. *An infinite regress of causes resulting in the existence of a particular thing is impossible.*

Therefore:

4. *There is a first cause of existence.*

It is apparent that the second way has a similar structure to the first way. Each argument has three premises, the first of which asserts a fairly simple fact that is verified by our experience of the world. Then come two premises, one asserting that no thing causes itself to change (first way) or to exist (second way); and the other denying the possibility of an infinite regress of causes of change (first way) or of existence (second way). Finally, we have the conclusion asserting that there exists an unchanging cause of change (first way) or an uncaused cause of existence (second way).

Before we take up Aquinas's rejection of the infinite regress of causes of existence, one important difference between the first and second way should be noted. We pointed out that a fundamental assumption underlies Aquinas's reasoning in the first way: namely, that, whenever a process of change occurs in a thing, something must cause that process of change. There can be no brute facts involving a process of change. The analogue to this assumption in the second way is that if something exists something must cause that thing to exist.

But no such assumption is required by Aquinas's reasoning in the second way. The reason for this is that the second premise of the second way is not "Whatever exists is caused to exist by something else" but "Whatever is caused to exist is caused to exist by something else." In order to prove the latter, all Aquinas need rule out is that something should be the cause of its own existence—and this he does by simply noting that if a thing caused its own existence it would have to precede itself, which, of course, is impossible.

We come again to the central issue in the first two ways: Aquinas's argument against an infinite regress of causes. The argument for this conclusion in the second way appears to be nothing more than a repetition of the question-begging argument we encountered in the first way. I suggested earlier, however, that there may be something more substantial beneath the surface of his argument against an infinite regress of causes; it is now time to pursue this matter.

The surface impression one gets from Aquinas's argument against the infinite regress of causes is that he holds that, whenever we have a series of causes of changes in existing things (first way) or a series of causes resulting in the existence of some thing (second way), the series must have a *first member*. Thus, for example, if one human being is generated by other human beings, and they in turn by still others, the impression his argument conveys is that each such series of generators of existence must stop with a first member, it cannot regress to infinity. But this is not Aquinas's view. Indeed, he explicitly rejects the view that the generation of one human by others could not proceed to infinity—"it is not impossible for a man to be generated by man to

22

infinity; . . ."[5] It is clear, then, that the impression given by Aquinas's argument against the infinite regress of causes does not represent his view. It must be that he thinks that only some regresses of causes cannot proceed to infinity. In order, then, to understand his argument, we need to distinguish those regresses of causes that he thinks may proceed to infinity from those he thinks cannot. Unfortunately Aquinas says little to help us in this matter. He does say that in efficient causes it is impossible to proceed to infinity per se, but possible to proceed to infinity accidentally as regards efficient causes.[6] Apparently, then, when we have a series of efficient causes, the series may be a per se series or an accidental series. If the former, it must have a first member; if the latter, it may proceed to infinity. The series of causes envisaged in the first and second ways must be per se series of causes. But just what does this distinction between per se and accidentally ordered causal series come to and why cannot there be an infinite regress in a per se series of causes?

Although, as I noted, Aquinas says little about what distinguishes the two series of causes, Duns Scotus lays down three features that he thinks distinguishes them. From what little Aquinas does say, it is fairly clear that he would accept the distinctions as Duns Scotus draws them.

> *Per se* or essentially ordered causes differ from accidentally ordered causes in three respects. The first difference is that in essentially ordered causes, the second depends upon the first precisely in its act of causation. In accidentally ordered causes this is not the case, although the second may depend upon the first for its

[5] ST, 1a. 46, 2.   [6] *Ibid.*

existence or in some other way. Thus a son depends upon his father for existence but is not dependent upon him in exercising his own causality, since he can act just as well whether his father be living or dead. The second difference is that in essentially ordered causes the causality is of another nature and order, inasmuch as the higher cause is more perfect. Such is not the case, however, with accidentally ordered causes. This second difference is a consequence of the first, since no cause in the exercise of its causality is essentially dependent upon a cause of the same nature as itself, for to produce anything one cause of a given kind suffices. The third difference is that all *per se* and essentially ordered causes are simultaneously required to cause the effect, for otherwise some causality essential to the effect would be wanting. In accidentally ordered causes this is not so, because there is no need of simultaneity in causing inasmuch as each possesses independently of the others the perfection of causality with regard to its own effect. For it is enough that one cause after the other exercises causality successively.[7]

The first and most fundamental difference, according to Duns Scotus, is that in an essentially (per se) ordered series of causes "the second depends upon the first precisely in its act of causation." The example, drawn from Aristotle, taken to exemplify this feature is that of the hand moving the staff, which in turn moves the stone. In this example, which Aquinas quotes in the first way, we are to view the hand as the first cause, the staff as an intermediate cause, and the stone as the last

[7] John Duns Scotus, *Philosophical Writings*, edited and translated by Allan Wolter (New York: Nelson and Sons, 1962), pp. 40-41.

effect in the series. Actually, it is not the stone's existence that is being caused in this series, but a change in the stone, a movement from one place to another. We are to imagine a man's hand, holding and moving a stick that is pressing against a stone and moving it. Now consider the act of the intermediate cause, i.e., the stick's moving and thereby causing the stone to move. Duns Scotus is saying that the intermediate cause, the stick, is dependent on its prior cause, the hand, *for its own causal activity*, i.e., moving the stone—and not dependent in some vague or general way, but "precisely in its act of causation." What causes the stick to be moving the stone is the hand and the fact that it is moving the stick. Contrast this essentially ordered series with the series involved in human generation. If man A causes the birth of man B, and man B causes the birth of man C, it is not true that what causes man B to give birth to C is man A and the fact that he caused B to exist. Of course, if A had not given birth to B, B (other things being equal) would not be giving birth to C. Similarly, if the hand had not moved the stick, the stick (other things being equal) would not have moved the stone. Granted this similarity in the two cases, there is still the profound difference that it is the hand's holding and moving the stick in a certain way that *causes* the stick to be moving the stone; whereas, it is not man A's causing man B to exist which *causes* man B to be giving birth to man C. As Aquinas remarks: "it is . . . accidental to this particular man as generator to be generated by another man; for he generates as a man and not as the son of another man." It is not, however, accidental to the stick as mover of the stone to be moved by the hand, for it is precisely the hand's moving the stick in a particular way that causes the stick to move the stone.

One by-product of this difference between the two series is that, in the essentially ordered series of the hand moving the stick which moves the stone, the causal relation is a *transitive relation*—that is, if the stone is being moved by the stick and the stick is being moved by the hand, it is also true that the stone is being moved by the hand. In the accidentally ordered series of human generation, the causal relation is not transitive—that is, if man C is generated by man B and man B is generated by man A, it is not also true that man C is generated by man A. A man is generated by his father, not by his grandfather. But the hand that moves the stick also moves the stone that is being moved by the stick.[8] According to Duns Scotus, then, in an essentially ordered series, the act of the first cause in causing the second *causes that very act* whereby the second causes the third, etc. And, as we saw, this allows us to say that the first causes the third.

Before considering the second and third distinctions that Duns Scotus draws between an essentially ordered series of causes and an accidentally ordered series, we should note one important implication of the first distinction for our understanding of the second way. Up to now we have been assuming that in the second way it is a thing's coming into existence that is the factor to be explained. But if we think of the causal series in which C is caused to come into existence by B, B by A, etc., the series in question will be an accidentally ordered series, for B's causing C to come into existence is

[8] A very illuminating discussion of the first feature by which Duns Scotus distinguishes the two series is to be found in Patterson Brown's "Infinite Causal Regression," *The Philosophical Review*, Vol. LXXV, No. 4 (October 1966), pp. 510-525. I am indebted to Brown's discussion.

not the direct effect of A's causing B to come into existence—as the case of human generation shows. Presumably Aquinas held that when a thing comes into existence there is an essentially ordered series of causes involved, but such a series would not proceed from C to B which caused C to come into existence, to A which caused B to come into existence, etc.

Thomistic scholars have suggested that it is not the *coming into existence* of a thing that Aquinas considers in the second way but the *present existence* of a thing.[9] Take any existing thing A, so the suggestion goes, there will be something B right now causing the existence of A from one moment to the next, causing A to continue existing rather than perish. Now the thing that is right now causing A to exist may also be being caused to be causing A to exist by something else C. C, let us say, causes B's present existence and causes B to be causing the present existence of A. It is perhaps useful here to think again of an essentially ordered series of causes in which the factor being caused is not the existence of a thing but some change in an existing thing, as, for example, when the stone is being moved. The hand causes the stick to be in motion and, in causing the stick to be in motion, causes the stick to be moving the stone. To consider the case in the second way, what C must do is cause B's present existence in such a way as to be causing B to be causing A's present existence—for unless B depends on C for its own causal activity vis-à-vis A's present existence, the causal series will not be essentially ordered and, therefore, will not be transitive in the sense that C may be said to be causing A's existence.

[9] See, for example, the discussion by Father Joyce in *The Principles of Natural Theology* (London: Longmans, Green and Co., 1934), pp. 58ff.

The basic point about the series of causes Aquinas is considering in the second way can be set forth as follows. We are to begin with some existing thing A, whose existence is being conserved by some other thing B. That is, B is causing A to continue existing; were B not conserving A in existence then, other things being equal, A would cease existing. Now B is either the first efficient cause of the causal series resulting in A's present existence or it is not. If it is not, then some further member of the series C is causing B to be causing A to exist. It is crucial here to note that what C does is not *simply* cause B to exist. For if this were so, the series from C to B to A could be an accidentally ordered series; it could be that C causes B's existence but does not cause B to be causing A to exist. The series is essentially ordered only if C causes B to be causing A to exist.

Having considered the first and most basic difference Duns Scotus draws between an essentially ordered and an accidentally ordered causal series and noted the implications of this for our understanding of the second way, we can now briefly consider the other two differences. In an essentially ordered series, the members of the series will differ in kind; whereas in an accidentally ordered series, they may be of the same kind. The latter point seems clear if we consider the accidentally ordered series of human generation. But since we do not yet have a clear example of an essentially ordered series of efficient causes of a thing's present existence, it is difficult to illustrate and evaluate the claim that the members of such a series must differ in kind and proceed from the less perfect to the more perfect.

The final distinguishing feature Duns Scotus notes is that members in an essentially ordered series are *simul-*

taneously active in bringing about their effect. This accords well with our first basic distinction. For, since the causal relation is transitive in an essentially ordered series, then if it is true that C causes B to cause A's present existence then it is true that C causes A's present existence. And if A would perish were not something presently conserving it, then C must be presently conserving A and, therefore, existing and exercising its causal activity simultaneously with A's existence.

If we bring together Duns Scotus's three distinguishing features as they apply to the second way, it seems we must understand Aquinas to be considering a causal series resulting in A's present existence such that (i) each member, B, C, etc., exercises its causal efficacy simultaneously with A's existence; (ii) as we proceed from A to B to C, etc., we proceed to beings of a different kind and higher order; and (iii) each higher member of the series is causing each lower member of the series to be causing the next lower to be causing until we arrive at that member, B, next to A, which simply causes A to be conserved in existence. Such a series is an essentially ordered series of efficient causes resulting in the present existence of A. And it is just such a series, as opposed to an accidentally ordered series, that Aquinas believes cannot proceed to infinity.

Before we reconsider why Aquinas rejects the infinite regress of causes in an essentially ordered series of efficient causes, we need to consider two points. First, when Aquinas says that something cannot cause its own existence because "this would mean it preceded itself, and this is not possible," he cannot mean that it would have to be *temporally* prior to itself. For, as we have just seen, the cause of A's present existence is causally active simultaneously with A's present existence. The causal series under consideration is one existing in the present, not stretching back into the past. The movement of the hand as it moves the stick is prior to the stick's movement in that it causes the stick's movement and not vice-versa. Presumably, then, Aquinas is rejecting the idea that a thing might cause its own continued existence on the grounds that the cause, if not always *temporally* prior to its effect, is, nevertheless, *causally* or perhaps *metaphysically* prior to it.

Second, we might well raise the question as to whether there is any good reason to believe that there are causal series of the sort Aquinas seems to be considering in the second way. It is true, of course, that there are any number of things on which I depend for my present existence—oxygen, heat, etc. But is it true that there is something that is causing me to exist right now, which in turn is being caused to cause me to exist right now, etc.? If we believe it is true, then we should be able to give a clear example of such a series, indicating specifically at least the first several things in the series resulting in my present existence. But in fact we hardly ever talk or think in terms of such a series. And when friendly expositors of Aquinas undertake to explicate the issue, they do little more than mention a necessary condition or two on which I am dependent for my present existence. Thus, for example, Father Copleston remarks:

> What he is thinking of can be illustrated in this way. A son is dependent on his father, in the sense that he would not have existed except for the causal activity of his father. But when the son acts for himself, he is not dependent here and now on his father. But he is dependent here and now on other factors. Without the

activity of the air, for instance, he could not himself act, and the life-preserving activity of the air is itself dependent here and now on other factors, and they in turn on other factors. I do not say that this illustration is in all respects adequate for the purpose; but it at least illustrates the fact that when Aquinas talks about an "order" of efficient causes he is not thinking of a series stretching back into the past, but of a hierarchy of causes, in which a subordinate member is here and now dependent on the causal activity of a higher member.[10]

In his discussion of the second way, Anthony Kenny notes that Aquinas thought that a series of simultaneous causes could be traced to the activity of the sun and other heavenly bodies.[11] Moreover, according to Kenny, Aquinas viewed the activty of the heavenly bodies as much more than mere necessary conditions for causal activities of earthly bodies. Since we no longer think this way, it is understandable why present-day interpreters of Aquinas have difficulty providing a clear example of an essentially ordered series of efficient causes resulting in the present existence of some thing. Indeed, Kenny rejects outright such a series with the remark that "the series of causes from which the Second Way starts is a series whose existence is vouched for only by medieval astrology."[12]

In defense of Aquinas, it may be argued that his basic belief that there is a series of essentially ordered causes responsible for the present existence of some object rests

[10] F. C. Copleston, *Aquinas* (Baltimore: Penguin Books, 1955), p. 118.

[11] *The Five Ways* (New York: Schocken Books, 1969), pp. 43-44.

[12] *Ibid.*, p. 44.

not on an acceptance of medieval astrology but on a metaphysical analysis of existence and causation. It may well be that, in giving an example of such a series, Aquinas would show dependence on some now-outdated empirical or quasi-empirical theory. But the existence of essentially ordered causal series would rest not on the correctness of some such "scientific" theory, but on metaphysical analysis and argument.

We come at last to the rejection of the infinite regress of causes, a rejection we now understand to be aimed only at an essentially ordered series of causes. As we noted earlier, Aquinas's argument appears to be a textbook example of begging the question. His argument is that, since to take away the cause is to take away the effect, if there were no first cause—as there would not be if the series went on to infinity—there would be no intermediate causes, and, consequently, no last effect. But since there clearly is a last effect—we see them all around us—there must be a first cause. Now this argument begs the very question at issue, for only in a series that has a first cause is it true that if you took *it* away you would take away all its effects. Hence, Aquinas is assuming that every series has a first member.

The interpretation of Aquinas's view that I propose is the following. Aquinas is *assuming* that there is or must be an explanation for the fact that causal activity of a certain sort is going on. This is the basic assumption that underlies the rejection of the infinite regress in both the first and the second way. In the first way, the kind of causal activity that is going on is that *causing a change in a particular thing A*; in the second way the kind of causal activity that is going on is that *causing the present existence of a certain thing A*. His point is that, if the series of essentially ordered causes proceeds

32

to infinity, does not terminate in a first member, there could be no explanation of the fact that a certain sort of causal activity is now going on. Let us see why this must be so.

Suppose B is now causing A to exist. Consider the fact that a certain sort of causal activity is now taking place, namely, the activity of causing A to exist. If B is the first member of the essentially ordered series resulting in A's present existence, then we might be able to explain the fact that this causal activity is now going on by reference to B. Suppose, however, that B is not the first member of the series but is itself now being caused to be causing A to exist by some other thing C. Can we now say that the explanation for the fact that the causal activity of causing A to exist is now going on might be found in B? It seems clear that we cannot. At this point, however, we must be careful to distinguish two different items:

> *i. the fact that A now exists,*

and

> *ii. the fact that a certain sort of causal activity (causing A to exist) is now going on.*

Someone might argue that, even though B is not the first member, we can still explain item (i) by reference to B and B's causal activity vis-à-vis A. I do not wish to dispute this point. To say that we have not really "explained" the present existence of A until we explain why B is causing A to exist, tracing each step backward until we arrive at an ultimate first cause, may be nothing more than a confusion as to the nature of explanation. But what we now want explained is not the present existence of A but the fact that a certain sort of causal

33

activity is occurring in the world. And it seems evident that if C is causing B to be exhibiting that causal activity, then we cannot explain the fact that that causal activity is now taking place by reference to B. Now if C is causing B to be causing A to exist, then since we are operating within an essentially ordered series it also will be true that C is now causing A to exist. C, therefore, will be exhibiting that very sort of causal activity we are trying to explain. And if C is the first member of the series, we might be able to explain why the causal activity *causing-A-to be now existing* is now going on by reference to C. However, if C is an intermediate cause, if some other thing is now causing C to be causing A to exist, then we cannot find the explanation for the fact that this activity is going on by reference to C. What then if the series progresses to infinity? Each member of the series will be right now exhibiting the causal activity we are trying to explain. It will be true that every member of the series is exhibiting the causal activity in question and also true that the fact that the causal activity is going on cannot be explained by any member of the series. For any member we select, it will be true that it is caused to exhibit the activity in question by some other member and, therefore, true that we cannot explain the fact that this sort of causal activity is going on in the universe by reference to that member.

Consider again Aristotle's example of an essentially ordered series of causes of change—the hand moving the stick that moves the stone. We must distinguish the fact that the stone is moving from the fact that a certain sort of causal activity—stone-moving activity—is now going on. Even though the stick is an intermediate cause, an instrument by means of which the hand moves the stone, someone might argue that the stick and the fact that it is moving and pushing against the stone is an explanation of the fact that the stone is moving. I do not wish to dispute this. But what we want to explain is the fact that stone-moving activity is now going on. Can we hope to explain this fact by reference to the stick? Clearly not. For since the stick is being caused to exhibit that activity by something else, since the stick would not be exhibiting that activity were not something else causing the stick to exhibit it, the fact that stone-moving activity is occurring in the world cannot be explained by reference to the stick. And so long as our regress of causes contains only members that are intermediate causes like the stick, there will be no explanation of the fact that this causal activity is now going on. And since, if the series progresses to infinity, each member will be like the stick, an intermediate cause, then if the series proceeds to infinity there will be no explanation of the fact that a certain sort of causal activity, causing stone moving, is going on in the world.

On the interpretation of Aquinas I am presenting, the present existence of A, its being conserved in existence, is the initial item of inquiry. But the item that will be left unexplained if the series of causes resulting in A's present existence stretches to infinity is not the present existence of A but the fact that a certain kind of causal activity is now going on, the causal activity resulting in the present existence of A. Where the item to be explained is not the fact that a particular thing A is now being conserved in existence but the fact that a certain sort of causal activity (causing A's present existence) is now going on, I have argued that the fact in question will be a brute fact, lacking an explanation, *if* the essentially ordered series of causes resulting in A's present existence proceeds to infinity, lacks a first mem-

35

ber. If this is correct, what bearing does it have on Aquinas's rejection of the infinite regress in an essentially ordered series of causes? As I noted earlier, on the interpretation I am proposing, we are to view Aquinas as assuming or taking for granted that there is or must be an explanation of the fact that a causal activity of a certain sort is going on. With this as given and the argument that I have just presented, we can conclude that every essentially ordered series of causes does have a first member, a member in which is to be found the explanation for the fact that the causal activity in question is going on. Put succinctly, the interpretation of Aquinas I am suggesting takes the following to be his basic argument against the infinite regress:

1. *Either every essentially ordered series of causes terminates in a first member that accounts for the fact that the causal activity exhibited by the members of the series is going on or there will be no explanation of the fact that that causal activity is going on.*
2. *There must be an explanation of the fact that a certain sort of causal activity is going on.*

Therefore:

3. *Every essentially ordered series of causes terminates in a first member which accounts for the fact that the causal activity exhibited by the members of the series is going on.*

It cannot reasonably be maintained that this argument is explicitly or implicitly contained in the argument Aquinas actually presents against the infinite regress of causes. That argument, whether taken from the first or second way, begs the question. I offer the above argument as a suggestion of what may underlie Aquinas's rejection of the infinite regress of causes. Apart from it or some argument like it, I cannot understand what reasons one could give for rejecting an infinite regress in an essentially ordered series of efficient causes.

To return to this argument, suppose someone questions the second premise. Why must the fact that the members of a series are exhibiting a certain causal activity have an explanation? Even if we admit that there is no necessity to that causal activity, that we can imagine that the world should have existed without it, why must the fact that it is occurring have an explanation? Perhaps it is simply a brute fact that there is a causal activity now going on that results in conserving A in existence. On what grounds can we reject the idea that the universe contains such unintelligible brute facts? Questions like these lead us to a fundamental metaphysical principle that is the moving force behind the Cosmological Argument, even when, as in the case of Aquinas's first and second ways, it does not appear in the statement of the argument. The principle in question is the Principle of Sufficient Reason, a principle that in its strongest form states that no thing can exist and no fact can obtain without there being an explanation for that thing's existence or for that fact's obtaining. Various forms of the Principle of Sufficient Reason will occupy our attention later in this study. It suffices here to note that some form of it lies behind the claim that the causal activity resulting in A's being conserved in existence must have an explanation.

Bringing together the results of our investigation of

Aquinas's first two ways, we may conclude that several assumptions play crucial roles in these arguments. In the first way it seems that Aquinas is assuming

> i. *that, if something is in a process of change, something must be causing it to be in that process of change;*
> ii. *that whatever is causing something to change toward a certain state must itself* actually *be in that state;*

and

> iii. *that if a certain causal activity is now going on which results in something being in a process of change, there must be an explanation of the fact that that causal activity is now going on.*

In the second way it seems that Aquinas is assuming

> iv. *that if a certain causal activity is now going on which results in something being conserved in existence, there must be an explanation of the fact that that causal activity is now going on.*

Our final judgment of these two arguments will depend on our assessment of these assumptions. As we have noted, the Principle of Sufficient Reason, if itself justified, would in turn justify several crucial assumptions that appear to underlie the reasoning exhibited in the first two ways. That principle, then, is the foundation on which the Cosmological Argument—at least the two versions we have thus far considered—rests. We shall examine that principle at some length in the next chapter, when we begin our consideration of the eighteenth-century form of the argument. For now it will suffice to note that, although the Principle of Sufficient

Reason does not appear explicitly in the reasoning exhibited in the first two ways, it, nevertheless, forms the basis for several crucial assumptions Aquinas makes in the course of developing his first two versions of the Cosmological Argument.

Aquinas's presentation of the third way is as follows:

The third way is based on what need not be and on what must be, and runs as follows. Some of the things we come across can be but need not be, for we find them springing up and dying away, thus sometimes in being and sometimes not. Now everything cannot be like this, for a thing that need not be, once was not; and if everything need not be, once upon a time there was nothing. But if that were true there would be nothing even now, because something that does not exist can only be brought into being by something already existing. So that if nothing was in being nothing could be brought into being, and nothing would be in being now, which contradicts observation. Not everything therefore is the sort of thing that need not be; there has got to be something that must be. Now a thing that must be, may or may not owe this necessity to something else. But just as we must stop somewhere in a series of causes, so also in the series of things which must be and owe this to other things. One is forced therefore to suppose something which must be, and owes this to no other thing than itself; indeed it itself is the cause that other things must be.[13]

Aquinas begins his argument by noting that there are things around us which "need not be." What he endeavors to prove first is that not everything that exists

[13] ST, 1a. 2, 3. I have again used the translation of the Blackfriars edition.

is of this "need not be" sort, that there is at least one thing that "must be." If we use the expression "necessary being" for Aquinas's "thing which must be," then what Aquinas starts from is the premise that there are things around us that are not necessary beings. Suppose we use the term "contingent being" to mean any existing being which is not a necessary being. If so, then we can say that Aquinas begins his argument with the observation that there are contingent beings, and he endeavors to prove first that not every existing being is contingent, that some existing being is necessary.

Before we pursue the details of his reasoning in the third way, we need to ask what Aquinas means by a necessary being," a being that "must be." It is now fairly well established that Aquinas does not mean a being whose non-existence is a logical impossibility.[14] Instead, he means a being in which there is no capacity for generation and no capacity for corruption. Aquinas held that many things in the world have a natural tendency toward corruption. These things are generated out of other things and over a period of time decay and pass away. Thus a contingent being for Aquinas is a being subject to the natural processes of generation and corruption; a necessary being, on the other hand, is a being in no way subject to generation and corruption. God, angels, the human soul, and the heavenly bodies are all necessary beings on Aquinas's view. To be a necessary being is not necessarily to be eternal or everlasting. A necessary being cannot come into existence by any *natural* process of generation or cease to exist by any *natural*

14 See Patterson Brown, "St. Thomas' Doctrine of Necessary Being," *The Philosophical Review*, Vol. LXXIII, No. 1 (January 1964), pp. 76-90. Also see Kenny, *The Five Ways*, pp. 47-48.

process of corruption. It may, nevertheless, be created *ex nihilo* by God and be annihilated by God.[15] In virtue of this conception of what "must be," Aquinas is led to consider whether a necessary being owes its necessity to something else. It is difficult to attach significance to the idea that a necessary being, in the sense of a being whose non-existence is a logical impossibility, might owe its necessity to another. But on the interpretation that Aquinas is working with, it makes perfectly good sense to raise the question. What, then, Aquinas is trying to prove in the third way is that there is a necessary being that owes its existence to no other thing, a being that has no cause of its necessity outside itself, but is rather the cause of necessity in other things.[16]

The structure of Aquinas's argument is as follows:

1. *There are contingent beings.*
2. *Not every being is a contingent being.*

Therefore:

3. *There exists a necessary being.*
4. *An infinite regress of necessary beings each having its necessity caused by another is impossible*

Therefore:

5. *There exists a necessary being which has its necessity of itself and not from another.*

[15] See Patterson Brown, "St. Thomas' Doctrine of Necessary Being."

[16] One important difference between the third way and the eighteenth-century form of the argument is that in the latter what is meant by "a necessary being" is a being whose non-existence is a logical impossibility.

The two critical steps in the argument are (2) and (4). In support of (2), Aquinas presents the following argument:

  i. Whatever is a contingent being at one time did not exist.

Therefore:

  ii. If everything is contingent then at one time nothing existed.
  iii. If at one time nothing existed then nothing would exist now.
  iv. Something does exist now.

Therefore:

  2. *Not every being is a contingent being.*

Against (i) it might be objected that to be contingent is to be generable and corruptible; but from this it does not follow that a contingent being was actually generated. Hence, it might always have existed. But presumably Aquinas means to hold that if something is inherently corruptible then it will in fact perish over some definite period of time. Hence, no contingent thing that now exists has always existed in the past, since it would have perished before now. Even if we concede (i) to Aquinas, however, the inference of (ii) from (i) is clearly invalid. From (i) it follows that if everything is contingent then for each thing there is a time at which it does not exist. That is, where $Cx = x$ is a contingent being, $Ty = y$ is a time, and $Exy = x$ exists at y, from (i) it follows that

  2a. $(x)(Cx \supset (\exists y)(Ty \ \& -Exy))$. *(Each contingent thing is such that there is some time or other when it did not exist.)*

But from (i) it does not follow that

2b. $(\exists y)\,(Ty\ \&\ (x)\,(Cx \supset\ -Exy))$. *(There is some definite time such that no contingent being existed at that time.)*

(2b) entails (2a), but is not entailed by (2a). Since (ii) asserts (2b) and since (2b) does not follow from (i), it seems clear that a crucial step in Aquinas's argument for the second premise "Not every being is a contingent being" involves a logical fallacy. This does not mean, of course, that the third way itself is a fallacious argument. We are here concerned not with the third way itself, but with an argument Aquinas uses to justify the truth of the second premise of the third way. We have just seen that that argument is fallacious. The third way itself, however, is a valid argument, its conclusion logically follows from its premises. Moreover, nothing we have thus far shown in any way implies that the second premise of the third way is defective. A fallacious argument can be given for a true proposition just as easily as for a false proposition. What we have shown is that Aquinas has failed to provide us with any good reasons for accepting the second premise of the third way. He has failed because the argument he advances for that premise commits a logical fallacy. The fallacy involves the reversal of quantifiers. Although $(\exists x)\,(y)\ Fxy$ entails $(y)\,(\exists x)\ Fxy$, the latter does not entail the former. Aquinas has fallaciously inferred a proposition of the general form of $(\exists x)\,(y)\ Fxy$ from a proposition of the form $(y)\,(\exists x)\ Fxy$.

It is sometimes suggested that there may be a plausible premise or principle that, when added to (i), will give us a logically valid inference to (ii). Father Copleston suggests, for example, that Aquinas is supposing that in an infinite time any real potentiality inevitably would be realized.[17] Accordingly, the questionable inference is not from (i) to (ii) but from (i) and the proposition that in an infinite time any real potentiality would be realized. The reasoning, on this suggestion, appears to be this. If every being were contingent, time would be infinite. Since each contingent being did not exist at one time, if every being were contingent, one real possibility would be that at a certain time none of them would exist. Now if time were infinite, this possibility would have been realized. Consequently, if every being were contingent, then at one time nothing existed.

Since the above reply to the objection that Aquinas's argument for (2) is fallacious has been carefully discussed in the literature, I shall not pursue the matter here.[18] There is, however, one step in Aquinas's argument for (2) that I do want to discuss since it reveals a rather basic assumption in Aquinas's argument that is important to bring to the surface. The third step in the argument for (2) is

iii. *If at one time nothing existed then nothing would exist now.*

The reason Aquinas gives for (iii) is simply that something comes into existence only through the causal activity of something already in existence. The principle expressed here implies that, if something comes into

17 *Aquinas* (Baltimore: Penguin Books, Inc., 1955), p. 120.

18 See, for example, Alvin Plantinga's *God and Other Minds* (Ithaca: Cornell University Press, 1967), pp. 3-25. For some remarks on Plantinga's discussion of the third way see my "God and Other Minds," *Nous*, Vol. III, No. 3 (September 1969), pp. 259-284.

existence, then there must be an explanation of its coming into existence. The explanation will involve reference to some other thing already in existence that caused it to come into existence. What Aquinas's argument requires us to believe is that the coming into existence of something cannot be a brute fact, a fact for which there is no explanation whatever. Again, then, a version of the Cosmological Argument is seen to depend on a principle requiring that there must be an explanation for any fact of a certain sort; namely, a fact consisting in something coming into existence.

Turning to the second part of the third way, we find the now familiar rejection of the infinite regress. Apparently Aquinas is prepared to advance the very same argument against the infinite regress that appears in the first two ways. If so, then the third way is subject to the major questions that were directed against Aquinas's rejection of the infinite regress in the first two ways. Since we have considered these questions in detail in connection with the second way, we need not consider further the justification Aquinas offers for the claim that an infinite regress of necessary beings, each having its necessity caused by another, is impossible.

What I have sought to show in this study of Aquinas's three versions of the Cosmological Argument is that, at crucial points in each way, an assumption is made to the effect that the fact that a thing exists, the fact that some thing comes into existence, or the fact that a certain kind of causal activity is going on in the world are facts for which there must be an explanation. These assumptions, I have suggested, reveal Aquinas's reliance on some general metaphysical principle that requires that such facts have an explanation. As we proceed with our study of the Cosmological Argument, we shall try to isolate the various forms this metaphysical principle might take and subject them to critical examination. For the moment it will suffice to note that some such metaphysical principle or principles provides the foundation for certain crucial assumptions at work in the first three ways.

The final thirteenth-century version of the Cosmological Argument we shall consider was developed by Duns Scotus.[19] As we shall see, Scotus's argument is quite different from the versions presented by Aquinas. Indeed, there is some question whether it is properly classified as a version of the Cosmological Argument. However, since his argument (i) endeavors to establish the existence of a first efficient cause, (ii) involves a rejection of an infinite causal regression, and (iii) appears to rest on some form of the Principle of Sufficient Reason, it is perhaps closer to the Cosmological Argument than to any other major classification of theistic arguments. In Duns Scotus's argument, however, there is no appeal to an observable fact about the world as its starting point. Instead, Scotus begins with a definition of a first efficient cause and a *modal* premise to the effect that the existence of a first efficient cause is a logical possibility. His reasoning purports to be entirely *a priori*. Thus, there are respects in which his argument resembles the arguments classified as versions of the Ontological Argument. For the reasons given, however, I shall here consider it as a form of the Cosmological Argument.

Scotus's argument consists of three steps, each of which is skillfully argued for:

> *I. It is possible that there exists a first efficient cause.*

[19] See *Duns Scotus: Philosophical Writings*, pp. 39-45.

II. *It is not possible that a first efficient cause be produced by something else.*

III. *A first efficient cause actually exists.*

By a "first efficient cause" Scotus means something that (a) is not produced by any other thing, and (b) does not exercise its causal efficacy in virtue of anything else. With this definition in mind, we can now consider Scotus's argument for I. His argument proceeds as follows:

1. *It is possible that something x exists that is produced.*
2. *If such an x existed it would not have produced itself or derived from nothing.*

Therefore:

3. *It is possible that an efficient cause y exists (from 1 and 2).*
4. *If y existed, it would either depend on another or would be a first efficient cause.*
5. *If y existed and depended on another, this other cause would be first or depend on another, etc.*

Therefore:

6. *If y existed, there would be either a first efficient cause, a circle of causes, or an infinite regress of causes.*
7. *A circle of causes is impossible.*
8. *An infinite regress of essentially ordered efficient causes is impossible.*

Therefore:

9. *It is possible that there exists a first efficient cause.*

Scotus's argument for step I is an *a priori* argument. His starting point is not that things exist that are caused to exist by other things, but only that it is *possible* that such things exist. Then, following a pattern of reasoning almost identical to Aquinas's reasoning in the second way, Scotus reaches his conclusion that it is possible that a first efficient cause exists. Although Scotus's argument for step I is familiar to us from our study of the second way, it is worth noting that in rejecting the infinite regress of causes Scotus does not simply repeat the question-begging argument Aquinas sets forth in the first two ways. Instead, he argues as follows:

> . . . in essentially ordered causes where our opponent assumes an infinity, the second of the series depends upon the first. This is a consequence of the first difference between essentially and accidentally ordered causes. Now if these causes were infinite so that not only would each single cause be posterior to something but every other cause which precedes it would be dependent in turn upon the cause that goes before it, then the whole series of effects would be dependent upon some prior cause. Now the latter cannot be a cause that is part of the series, for then it would be its own cause. The series as a whole, then, is dependent on something which does not pertain to the group that is caused, and this I call the first efficient cause. Even if the group of beings caused were infinite, they would still depend upon something outside the group.[20]

Although Scotus's argument is undoubtedly subject to several interpretations, I think it squares rather well with the view I have attributed to Aquinas. Suppose the series goes to infinity, does not terminate in a first

[20] *Ibid.*, pp. 41-42.

member, then the fact that the kind of causal activity exhibited by each member of the series is now going on will be a *brute fact,* a fact without explanation. If we ask the question "Why is it that there is an infinite series of causes, each one now exhibiting this sort of causal activity?" there will be no answer to our question. Suppose we say with Scotus that something must account for why each member of the series is exhibiting this sort of causal activity. Could that thing itself be a part of the series? Clearly not. For if it were, then since, as part of the series, it is being caused to exhibit the causal activity in question, then if by virtue of its own causal activity it explains why the things in the series are exhibiting the causal activity in question, it would be *its own cause.* So long, then, as we suppose that there must be an explanation for the fact that a causal series exists in which each member is caused to be exhibiting a certain activity by a preceding member, then we must either have a finite series terminating in a first member or admit that there is something outside of the infinite series that explains why the whole infinite series of things is exhibiting the activity in question. Whether the series is finite or infinite, there must, then, be a first efficient cause.

Perhaps a distinction will help us understand Scotus's argument. By saying that a certain causal series is *infinite* we might mean

   a. *that there is no first thing that accounts for the members in the series but is not itself accounted for by something else,*

or,

   b. *that there is an infinite number of causes prior to a particular effect.*

49

When Scotus rejects the infinite regress of essentially ordered causes, he means to be rejecting (a) not (b). In fact, in his argument he seems to allow that there might be an infinite number of essentially ordered causes prior to a particular effect. Even allowing this, however, we still will have to postulate a first cause outside of the series to account for the whole series. For if we do not postulate such a first cause, then there will be an unexplained brute fact: namely, that the entire series is exhibiting a certain causal activity. Thus, it seems to me that what Scotus says about the infinite regress of essentially ordered causes is consistent with, if not supportive of, the interpretation we pursued in connection with Aquinas's argument in the second way. In each case there is a reliance on the Principle of Sufficient Reason to rule out the apparent possibility that the regress of causes might simply be a brute fact without any explanation.

Many philosophers would be prepared to concede step I to Duns Scotus without requiring a lengthy argument. Indeed, the premise in which Scotus rejects an infinite regress of essentially ordered causes strikes me as a good deal more suspect than the conclusion he wants to prove: namely, that it is logically possible that something exists that is not produced by any other thing and that is not being caused by something else to exhibit its causal activity. Surely there is no logical absurdity in the idea of a first efficient cause. Hence, even though we may find premises in Scotus's argument that are uncertain or in some way suspect, the conclusion of the argument seems altogether plausible, if not completely beyond suspicion. Let us then concede the mere possibility of a first efficient cause and proceed to the last two steps in Scotus's Cosmological Argument.

Step II—that it is not possible that a first efficient cause be produced by something else—is, if anything, more certain and evident than step I. For, given Scotus's definition of "a first efficient cause" as, in part, something that is not produced by any other thing, the following sentence appears to express a contradiction: "Some first efficient cause is produced by something else." If so, Scotus is surely right in concluding that it is not possible that a first efficient cause be produced by something else. Step II, like step I, may be conceded to Duns Scotus without requiring supporting arguments.

We come now to the final stage of Scotus's Cosmological Argument, the argument for step III. This argument consists of three premises: step I, step II, and the following principle: "Anything to whose nature it is repugnant to receive existence from something else, exists of itself if it is able to exist at all." How are we to interpret Scotus's principle? I suggest the following:

> A. If it is possible for x to exist, then if x does not actually exist it is possible for x to be produced by something else.[21]

Given A and steps I and II it logically follows that a first efficient cause actually exists. For if we replace "x" in (A) by "a first efficient cause" (A) becomes

> A'. If it is possible for a first efficient cause to exist then if a first efficient cause does not actually

[21] This interpretation of Scotus's principle is logically equivalent to the interpretation provided by the Scotist scholar Efrem Bettoni in *Duns Scotus: The Basic Principles of His Philosophy*, translated by Bernardine Bonansea (Washington, D.C.: The Catholic University of America Press, 1961), p. 141. Bettoni's interpretation is: "if the first cause does not exist, it is causable, since it is possible."

exist it is possible for a first efficient cause to be produced by something else.

Now from A′ and step I we infer that if a first efficient cause does not actually exist it is possible for a first efficient cause to be produced by something else. And from this last and step II, it follows that a first efficient cause actually exists. Since we have conceded steps I and II to Scotus, we must also concede step III—that there actually exists a first efficient cause—unless we are to fault principle (A).

Principles similar to (A) appear in the arguments of other medieval philosophers. Anselm, for example, in his response to Gaunilo, gives an argument for the existence of God in which a principle similar to (A) is employed: namely,

B. *If x does not exist and it is possible that x exist, then it is possible for x to come into existence.*

Since it is impossible for God to come into existence and since His existence is possible, it follows, so Anselm reasons, that God actually exists.

Against principles (A) and (B) we may advance the following counter-example. Surely it is possible for an everlasting star to exist. The stars that exist are presumably not everlasting—for each star, let us suppose, there was a time before which it did not exist and there will be a time at which it ceases to exist. But this seems to be an empirical fact and not a matter of conceptual or logical necessity. The idea of an everlasting star does seem to be a non-contradictory idea, even if no star is in fact everlasting. Let us grant, then, that

i. *it is possible for an everlasting star to exist.*

Now clearly we must grant that

> ii. *it is impossible for an everlasting star to come into existence. (If x comes into existence then by definition x is not everlasting.)*

Moreover, since if something is produced by something else then there was a time before which it did not exist, we have

> iii. *it is impossible for an everlasting star to be produced by something else.*

Now suppose it is true, as we believe, that no star in existence is everlasting. If so, then principles (A) and (B) are false. For given (i), (ii), (iii), and either (A) or (B), it follows that an everlasting star actually exists. The strategy, then, for refuting (A) and (B) is to select some object x that we know does not exist but whose everlasting existence is a logical possibility. We then consider the idea of an everlasting x. It will then be possible that an everlasting x exist, impossible that an everlasting x is produced or comes into existence, and false that an everlasting x exists. Principles (A) and (B), therefore, are false.[22]

---

[22] These counter-examples against (A) and (B) are legitimate so long as the modal constituents of (A) and (B) are read *de dicto*, rather than *de re*. If read *de re*, it can be argued that it is possible for an everlasting star to be produced and to come into existence. For the duration of a star's existence does not seem to be an essential feature of its nature. Consequently, that star that happens to be everlasting *might* have come into existence or have been produced. Compare, for example, the proposition "It is not possible that the bachelor next door is married." Read *de dicto* the proposition is true, read *de re* it is false. It may be, then, that

We have been considering Duns Scotus's argument for the existence of a first efficient cause. His argument and Aquinas's first three ways constitute a high-water mark in the history of the Cosmological Argument. They express the major forms of the argument in the thirteenth century. In the rest of this study, we shall be concerned mainly with the form the argument took in the eighteenth century, the second high-water mark in the historical development of the argument. As I expressed earlier, it is my belief that the most sophisticated and fully developed form of the argument is the eighteenth-century version developed by Samuel Clarke in his Boyle lectures delivered in 1704. I shall not try directly to justify this belief in the course of this study. That it is justified will be apparent, I hope, to the reader when he comes to grips with Clarke's argument and compares it with the historically significant versions of the argument we have just considered. My claim, however, is not that Clarke's argument is necessarily a more cogent argument than, say, Aquinas's second way. Rather it is that Clarke's argument is a more fruitful argument for philosophical study insofar as we are concerned to study the fundamental concepts and principles at work in the Cosmological Argument. Although I hope this too will become apparent to the reader as he considers the eighteenth-century form of the argument, three brief remarks here may indicate some of my reasons for this judgment.

The impression one gains from the thirteenth-century forms of the Cosmological Argument is that a central feature of the argument is the rejection of the idea that

---

more would have to be said in refutation of (A) and (B) than I have here said. I shall not, however, pursue this matter further here.

every existing thing could have the status of an intermediate cause, that is, a cause that is itself caused by something else. This impression, I think, is absolutely correct. The rejection of the idea that everything has or might have the status of an intermediate cause is an essential feature of the Cosmological Argument for the existence of God. This impression, however, is obscured in the thirteenth-century versions by a further impression: in order to argue successfully against the view that everything might have the status of an intermediate cause, we must focus on a rather strange causal series, an essentially ordered series of causes. For, as I have argued, the thirteenth-century argument against the infinite regress of essentially ordered causal series requires a form of the Principle of Sufficient Reason as a foundation for some of the crucial assumptions in that argument. But, given the Principle of Sufficient Reason, we can argue just as successfully by considering the kind of causal series we are most familiar with: namely, causal series stretching backward in time. The justification for this claim must await our study of the eighteenth-century form of the argument. That form of the argument, as we shall see, in no way requires that we distinguish essentially ordered from accidentally ordered causal series and focus our attention only on the former. Any causal series will do as a basis for arguing that not everything can have the status of an intermediate cause. And if this is so, as I think it is, then the Cosmological Argument is freed from reliance on what many philosophers would regard as a strange and perhaps non-existent kind of causal series. Since I think this is so, I am led to the view that the eighteenth-century form of the argument, as presented by Samuel Clarke, is a more fruitful version for sustained study insofar as we are trying to isolate the essential features of the Cosmological Argument.

A second reason why the eighteenth-century form of the Cosmological Argument is particularly helpful in enabling us to come to grips with the essential features of the Cosmological Argument is that the Principle of Sufficient Reason, which we have seen to be the foundation of several important assumptions in the thirteenth-century versions, is explicitly a part of the eighteenth-century form of the argument and is explicitly discussed by that argument's most important proponents, Leibniz and Samuel Clarke. Since that principle is essential to the Cosmological Argument, it is extremely useful in studying the argument to consider how the proponents of the argument actually formulate the principle, how they use it in developing the Cosmological Argument, and what they say in behalf of the principle. These matters are all reasonably close to the surface in Clarke's presentation of the Cosmological Argument; whereas they tend to lie beneath the surface in the versions of the argument presented by Aquinas and Duns Scotus.

Finally, the major objections set forth against the Cosmological Argument in the modern period—objections advanced by Hume, Russell, and others—have been leveled at the eighteenth-century form of the argument. To assess the merits of these objections, we must consider in depth the version of the argument to which they are directed. Moreover, since it is fair to say that those philosophers in the modern period who reject the argument are persuaded to do so mainly by the sorts of objections advanced by Hume and Russell, our study will be more relevant to the contemporary philosophical scene if we make the eighteenth-century form of the argument the major focus of our study.

Having examined the important thirteenth-century forms of the argument and having briefly explained why in the rest of this study we shall concentrate our attention mainly on the eighteenth-century form of the argument, we can bring this chapter to a close by indicating just how we shall proceed in the succeeding parts of this study.

Clarke's important work, *A Demonstration of the Being and Attributes of God*, consists of twelve propositions and arguments in support of these propositions. The first three propositions and their arguments constitute the first part of the Cosmological Argument.[23] The arguments for the first three propositions are designed to establish the existence of a *necessary being*.[24] Propositions IV to XII and their arguments constitute the second part of the Cosmological Argument. The arguments for these propositions are designed to establish

[23] Although the argument (the Leibniz-Clarke argument) we shall examine is only one *version* of the Cosmological Argument, for convenience I shall frequently speak of this argument as the Cosmological Argument.

[24] Scholars have observed that in Part IX of his *Dialogues Concerning Natural Religion* Hume has Demea advance an argument that is a brief restatement of certain portions of the argument Clarke developed in his Boyle lectures. Indeed, Wollheim thinks it probable that Demea is to be identified with Samuel Clarke. See *David Hume on Religion*, edited with an introduction by Richard Wollheim (Cleveland: The World Publishing Company, 1964), p. 21. Norman Kemp Smith remarks that Demea's argument is a brief restatement of the argument formulated by Clarke. See David Hume, *Dialogues Concerning Natural Religion*, edited with an introduction by Norman Kemp Smith (Indianapolis: The Bobbs-Merrill Co., 1947), p. 115. Hume himself refers to Clarke in a footnote. It is important to note, however, that the argument Hume puts into Demea's mouth represents only the *first part* of Clarke's Cosmological Argument.

that the necessary being whose existence has been established (Propositions I, II, and III) is incomprehensible
in its essence (Prop. IV); is such that some of its attributes, e.g., eternality, can be demonstrated (Prop. V);
is endowed with liberty and choice (Prop. IX); is omnipotent (Prop. X); is infinitely good (Prop. XI), etc. That
is, taken together, the arguments for Propositions IV to
XII are designed to show that the necessary being is
God.[25]

In the next three chapters I shall be concerned with
the concepts and theses essential to the reasoning exhibited in the *first part* of the Cosmological Argument,
i.e., the argument for the existence of a necessary being.
As we noted, Clarke develops this part of the Cosmological Argument in three steps. In the first step, he
endeavors to establish that there never was a time when
nothing existed. In Chapter II, we shall examine the
arguments Clarke gives for this claim and bring to light
the key principle employed in his reasoning: namely,
the Principle of Sufficient Reason. We shall then consider this principle in detail, distinguish weaker and
stronger forms of it, and consider whether it can be
shown to be true or false.

[25] I noted earlier that much less criticism has been directed at
the second part of the Cosmological Argument than has been
directed at the first. One notable instance of philosophical criticism directed at the second part of the argument is to be found
in the correspondence of Bishop Butler. Butler, who was a student when Clarke's *Demonstration* was published, in a series of
five letters—Clarke responded to each letter—criticized both
Clarke's proof for the infinity of the necessary being (Prop. VI)
and his proof that there could be only one necessary being (Prop.
VII). This correspondence was appended to later editions of
Clarke's *A Demonstration of the Being and Attributes of God.*
For further discussion of the Butler-Clarke correspondence, see
Chapter V, pp, 229-232.

In the second step of his argument for the existence of a necessary being, Clarke tries to establish that there exists an *independent* being, a being that has the reason for its existence within its own nature. In Chapter III, we shall consider the reasoning Clarke gives for this claim and examine in detail the two major criticisms philosophers have advanced against that reasoning.

In Chapter IV, we shall consider the final step of Clarke's argument for the existence of a necessary being and examine a number of issues related to the concept of a necessary being. In Chapter V, we shall consider the second part of the Cosmological Argument, the arguments by which Clarke hopes to establish that the necessary being, whose existence has been established in the first part, has the properties of the theistic God. Finally, in a concluding chapter we shall assess the strengths and weaknesses of the Cosmological Argument as a proof of, or acceptable argument for, the existence of God.

II

The Cosmological Argument and the Principle of Sufficient Reason

THE first proposition Clarke endeavors to prove is: "Something has existed from eternity." Before considering his arguments, we may note first that Clarke also uses the sentence "Something always was" to express Proposition I. Second, as shall become clear in the discussion of Proposition II, Clarke here means to prove not that some *one* being has always existed, but only the more modest claim that for every past moment *some being or other* (i.e., not necessarily the same being) has been in existence.[1] Hence, his first

---

[1] There is, I think, an ambiguity in the sentence "Something always was" that Clarke fails to notice. As I have indicated, he appears to use the sentence "Something always was" to express the proposition: A. *For every past moment of time some being or other has been in existence.* But "Something always was" also might be used to express the proposition: B. *There never was a moment in time when it was true that for every previous moment nothing was in existence.* A and B are not logically equivalent. Although A entails B, B does not entail A. For B does not preclude there being moments in which nothing exists. Clarke's argument, I think, establishes B but not A. To establish A, we would require the further premise that if *x* exists by reason of the causal efficacy of some being *y* existing temporally prior to *x*, it is not true that any time elapsed between *y*'s ceasing to exist and *x*'s coming into existence. In terms of the later development of his argument all he needs to establish is B. Consequently, it will not

proposition is consistent with the proposition that each being is such that at some moment or other it did not exist. Of course, his first proposition is also consistent with the proposition that some one being has always existed. Third, immediately after stating Proposition I, "Something has existed from eternity," Clarke makes the curious remark: "This is so evident and undeniable a proposition, that no atheist in any age has ever presumed to assert the contrary; and therefore there is little need of being particular in the proof of it." As we shall see, Clarke is not very particular in the proof of it. Indeed, his first argument is not a proof, and his second argument contains a premise that is considerably stronger than is needed to derive the proposition in question.

Clarke's statement of his first argument for Proposition I is:

> For since something now is, it is evident that something always was: otherwise the things that now are, must have been produced out of nothing, absolutely and without cause: which is a plain contradiction in terms. For, to say a thing is produced, and yet that there is no cause at all of that production, is to say that something is effected, when it is effected by nothing; that is, at the same time when it is not effected at all (*Demonstration*, pp. 8-9).

The argument expressed in this passage may be stated as follows:

1. Something now exists.

2. If something now exists and it is not the case

---

matter here whether we introduce this further premise into his argument and take "Something always was" as expressing A *or*

> *that something has always existed then some-*
> *thing has been produced out of nothing.*
> 3. *The proposition "Something has been produced*
> *out of nothing" is a contradiction.*

Therefore:

> 4. *Something has always existed.*

This argument is certainly valid; the conclusion, Proposition I, clearly follows from the premises. But is the
argument sound? That is, are all its premises true? I very
much doubt that this is so. Although (1) is surely true,
and (2) seems to be a necessary truth, it is far from
clear that (3) is true. What is clear, I think, is that the
argument Clarke gives to show that (3) is true is a bad
argument. His argument for (3) may be expressed as
follows:

> *3a. "Something has been produced out of nothing"*
> *entails "Something has been produced and not*
> *produced."*

Therefore:

> 3. *"Something has been produced out of nothing"*
> *is a contradiction.*

This argument, like the main argument, is certainly
valid. "Something has been produced and not produced" is clearly a contradiction, and any proposition
that entails a contradiction must itself be a contradiction. The difficulty is that the premise, (3a), is false. It
is false because, although "Something has been produced out of nothing" entails "Something has not been

---

leave his argument as is but take "Something always was" as
expressing B.

produced," it surely does *not* entail "Something has been produced." To say "Something has been produced out of [by] nothing" is to say no more than "Something exists which has not been produced." If I say of something, a stone, for example, that nothing produced it, I certainly am not saying—nor does what I say entail—that the stone *was produced*. What I am saying of the stone is that it was not produced at all.

The fact that Clarke's argument in support of (3) is unsound does not, of course, entitle us to conclude that (3) is false. (3) *may* be true. But it is not necessary to know that (3) is false, or even to claim that (3) is false, in order to show that in arguing from premises (1), (2), and (3) to the conclusion, (4), Clarke has failed to *prove* that something has always existed. For, in using this argument, Clarke has thereby *proved* its conclusion only if he *knows* that each premise is true. And, as we have just seen, the only reason he seems to have for holding that (3) is true is the fact that it is entailed by (3a). But, since (3a) is false, it cannot enable Clarke to know the truth of any proposition entailed by it. Therefore, since the sole reason Clarke here gives in support of (3) cannot possibly enable him to *know* that (3) is true, and since he has succeeded in *proving* the conclusion, (4), only if he knows that each of the premises of his argument for (4) is true, we are, I believe, justified in concluding that Clarke has not, by means of his first argument, *proved* what he has undertaken to prove— namely, that something has existed from eternity.

Immediately following what I have taken to be the statement of his first argument for Proposition I, Clarke expresses what appears to be a second argument. He says,

Whatever exists has a cause, a reason, a ground of its existence; (a foundation, on which its existence relies;) either in the necessity of its own nature, and then it must have been of itself eternal: or in the will of some other being; and then that other being must, at least in the order of nature and causality, have existed before it (*Demonstration*, p. 9).

This is a perplexing passage; but it contains, I believe, Clarke's major argument for Proposition I. As a first step toward stating the argument here expressed, I suggest the following:

1. Something now exists.

2. If something exists then either it exists by reason of the necessity of its own nature or it exists by reason of the causal efficacy of some other being.

3. If something exists by reason of the necessity of is own nature then it always has existed.

4. If something exists by reason of the causal efficacy of some other being then that other being has existed before it.

Therefore:

5. Something always has existed.

Several comments need to be made concerning this argument. First it must be acknowledged that it is far from clear what is or could be meant by the sentence "Something exists by reason of the necessity of its own nature." But, since Clarke attempts to clarify the meaning of this sentence in connection with his discussion of Proposition III, I shall defer consideration of this problem until we examine his arguments for Proposition III. For now, I shall assume—what Clarke later argues for—that the meaning of "has the reason of its existence within its own nature" is such that any being that does have the reason of its existence within its own nature *must* be an eternal being.

Second, the validity of Clarke's argument results from the *recursive* application of premises (2), (3), and (4). That this is so can be shown in the following way. Suppose, to satisfy premise (1), we select some presently existing being *a*. Either *a* exists by reason of the necessity of its own nature or it does not. If it does, then by premise (3) it will follow that *a* always has existed. If it does not, then from premises (2) and (4) it follows that some other being *b* caused *a* to exist, and existed at some time prior to when *a* existed. But premises (2), (3), and (4), if true at all, apply to *b* as well as to *a*. The same reasoning we just went through concerning *a* now applies to *b*. Thus it will follow that either *b* always has existed or some other being *c* caused *b* to exist and existed at some time prior to when *b* existed. By the recursive application of premises (2), (3), and (4)—even if no being exists by reason of the necessity of its own nature—it will follow that no being exists at a time such that for every preceding moment nothing exists. For, suppose that some being *n* existed at time *t* but for every moment prior to *t* nothing existed. From this supposition and premise (3), it will follow that *n* does not exist by reason of the necessity of its own nature. And, if that is so, from premises (2) and (4) we can conclude that some other being *m* caused *n* to exist and existed at some moment prior to any moment when *n* exists. But this conclusion is incompatible with our assumption that *n* existed at *t* and nothing existed prior to *t*. Hence, since this supposition has been shown to be incompatible with the premise set (2), (3), and (4), and since something does exist (premise 1), we may conclude that (5) something always has existed.

There is, I think, a difficulty in the reasoning just presented. Suppose some being a is caused to exist by a_1, a_1 by a_2, a_2 by a_3, etc. Suppose some *finite* interval of time t to t-20 is such that a exists at t but not at t-10; a_1 at t-10 but not at t-15; a_2 at t-15 but not at t-17½, etc. Prior to t-20, no being has ever existed. But it is not true that there is any being a_i such that for every unit of time prior to when a_i exists nothing was in existence. There is an infinite number of beings in the interval t to t-20 and each is such that the being that caused it exists prior to it.

The state of affairs just depicted satisfies Clarke's premises but falsifies his conclusion. The premises do establish that for every being that is not eternal there is some being that exists prior in time to it. What they do not establish is that there never was a moment of time such that for every moment prior to it nothing existed. For if we select the moment t-21 it will be true that prior to it nothing existed.

The Cosmological Argument itself, I think, is not subject to this objection. But Clarke's argument for Proposition I is subject to it. To avoid this objection, I suggest we concede to Clarke the additional premise that there is some *definite, finite interval of time* (as small as you wish) such that for any (non-eternal) beings x and y if x causes y to exist then x existed prior to y for at least that finite time interval.

Although with the addition of this further premise, the recursive application of premises (2), (3), and (4) in conjunction with premise (1) yields the conclusion (5), there is a problem of some importance concerning premise (4) and the manner in which I have interpreted it. Premise (4), according to my statement of it, is the proposition:

> *If something exists by reason of the causal efficacy of some other being then that other being has existed before it.*

In the passage quoted from Clarke, however, the *complete* statement of this premise would seem to be as follows:

> *If something exists by reason of the causal efficacy of some other being then that other being—at least in the order of nature and causality—has existed before it.*

The problem here is to explain what Clarke means by the added qualification "at least in the order of nature and causality."

I believe that Clarke introduces this qualification to allow for the possibility that a being might always have existed and, nevertheless, exist by reason of the causal efficacy of some other being. As he later notes, some philosophers in antiquity (he mentions both Plato and Aristotle) seem to have held that the world may be both eternal and caused by God. Thus in discussing Plato's view of creation, he remarks:

> At least his followers afterward so understood and explained it, as if by the creation of the world was not to be understood a creation in time; but only in order of nature, causality and dependence: That is; that the will of God, and his power of acting, being necessarily as eternal as his essence; the effects of that will and power might be supposed coeval to the will and power themselves; in the same manner, as Light would eter-

nally proceed from the Sun, or a shadow from the interposed body, or an impression from an imposed seal, if the respective causes of these effects were supposed eternal (*Demonstration*, p. 35).

Although Clarke certainly believes that the world is not eternal, he nowhere argues that its having a cause entails that it is not eternal. Indeed, he seems to hold a view not unlike that of Aquinas, namely, that although unaided reason can demonstrate that the world is created it cannot prove that the world is not eternal. Thus in his discussion of Proposition III Clarke remarks:

That the material world is not self existent or necessarily existing, but the product of an intelligent and wise agent, may (as I have already shown) be strictly demonstrated by bare reason against the most obstinate atheism in the world: but the time when the world was created; or whether its creation was, properly speaking, in time; is not so easy to demonstrate strictly by bare reason, (as appears from the opinions of many of the ancient philosophers concerning that matter,) but the proof of it ought to be taken from revelation (*Demonstration*, pp. 36-37).[2]

[2] Aquinas remarks: "*I answer that,* That the world did not always exist we hold by faith alone: it cannot be proved demonstratively; . . ." (ST, 1a, q. 46, 2). Aquinas also endeavors to explain how it is possible for something that always has existed to, nevertheless, have its cause in some other being.

To understand this we must consider that an efficient cause which acts by motion of necessity precedes its effect in time; for the effect exists only in the end of the action, and every agent must be the beginning of action. But if the action is instantaneous and not successive, it is not necessary for the maker to be prior in duration to the thing made, as appears in the case of illumination. Hence it is held that it does not follow necessarily

When Clarke says that if a being has the cause of its existence in some other being "that other being must, at least in the order of nature and causality, have existed before it," he means, I think, to express in a single proposition what we may, for purposes of clarity, express by the following two propositions:

a. *If some being has always existed and exists by reason of the causal efficacy of some other being then that other being must have existed before it only in the order of nature, causality, and dependence.*

b. *If some being has not always existed and exists by reason of the causal efficacy of some other being then that other being must have existed at some time before it.*

If this is correct, it follows that the proposition I listed as premise (4)—"If something exists by reason of the causal efficacy of some other being then that other being has existed before it" does not adequately express Clarke's view. For, interpreting "before" as *temporally before*, it would follow that no eternal being could have the cause of its existence in some other being. Indeed, from premises (4) and (2) it would follow that every eternal being exists by reason of the necessity of its own nature. But, as we have seen, although Clarke thinks it demonstrable that the world has its cause in some other

---

that if God is the active cause of the world, He must be prior to the world in duration; because creation, by which He produced the world, is not a successive change, as was said above. (ST, 1a, q. 46, 1, ad. 1)

From this passage and others, it is clear that Aquinas held that the two concepts *caused by God* and *always existing* are not incompatible.

being (i.e., God), he does not think it demonstrable that the world is temporally finite. For that belief he, like Aquinas, appears to rely on divine revelation.

In view of the above, we may now state a simple but, nevertheless, accurate expression of the major argument Clarke gives in support of Proposition I, "Something has existed from eternity."

1. *Something now exists.*
2. *If something exists then either it exists by reason of the necessity of its own nature or it exists by reason of the causal efficacy of some other being.*
3. *If something exists by reason of the necessity of its own nature then it always has existed.*
4. *If something exists by reason of the causal efficacy of some other being then unless it has always existed that other being must have existed temporally prior to it.*

Therefore:

5. *Something always has existed.*

The proposition I have just used as premise (4) allows for the possibility that an eternal being may have the cause of its existence in some other being—in which case the cause will not exist *temporally* prior to its effect but will be prior *only* in the order of nature, causality, and dependence.

I said above that this argument contains a premise that is a good deal stronger than what is required in order for the conclusion to be derived. The premise in question is (2), "If something exists then either it exists by reason of the necessity of its own nature or it exists by reason of the causal efficacy of some other being." It is clear why Clarke does not employ the following proposition in the place of (2):

> *If something exists then it exists by reason of the causal efficacy of some other being.*

For this proposition is incompatible with the existence of the being (God) that the Cosmological Argument purports to establish. God is an eternal, independent being; other things exist by reason of God's causal efficacy, but God does not have the cause of his existence in any other being. However, if all that needs proving is that something always has existed, it is clear that the following proposition, which is less complex and more plausible than (2), will suffice.

> *If something comes into existence then it exists by reason of the causal efficacy of some other being.*

Given this proposition, we may construct a much simpler and more plausible argument than Clarke's for Proposition 1.

1. *Something now exists.*
2. *If something exists then either it has always existed or it has come into existence.*
3. *If something comes into existence then it exists by reason of the causal efficacy of some other being.*
4. *If something exists by reason of the causal efficacy of some other being then unless it has always existed that other being must have existed temporally prior to it.*

Therefore:

5. *Something always has existed.*

71

This argument, like Clarke's, does not preclude the possibility that an eternal being has the cause of its existence in some other being. But, unlike Clarke's, it avoids use of the obscure phrase "exists by reason of the necessity of its own nature," and requires a cause only for things that come into existence. Unlike Clarke's argument, no claim is made that there must be an explanation for the existence of absolutely every existing thing, even an eternal being. Only the more modest claim is made—namely, that whatever *begins to exist* must have a cause or reason of its existence. The conclusion, "Something has always existed," however, follows from this simpler, more plausible premise set, just as it does from Clarke's more complex and less plausible premise set.

The question as to why Clarke uses a substantially stronger premise set than is necessary for the derivation of Proposition I can, I think, be answered. This question, in effect, is the question as to why Clarke employs the premise that *whatever exists* must have an explanation of its existence, rather than the more modest premise that *whatever comes into existence* must have an explanation of its existence. Even though the latter claim, in conjunction with the other premises, suffices for the derivation of Proposition I, the reason Clarke employs the much stronger claim is—as will be apparent when we consider his argument for Proposition II— that only the stronger claim will enable him to argue for the existence of a necessary being. Hence, although Clarke could have used the weaker proposition "Whatever comes into existence must have an explanation of its existence" to justify Proposition I, only the stronger proposition "Whatever exists must have an explanation of its existence" will suffice for establishing Propositions II and III.

My purpose in constructing a simpler argument for Proposition I is to bring to light two different versions of what is frequently called *The Principle of Sufficient Reason*—hereafter referred to as PSR. According to the strong version of PSR, whatever exists must have an explanation of its existence—either in the necessity of its own nature or in the causal efficacy of some other being. According to the weak version of PSR, whatever comes into existence must have an explanation of its existence. The explanation of its existence will lie in the causal efficacy of some other being. The Cosmological Argument—at least Clarke's version of it—requires the strong version of PSR.

Can PSR in its strong form be proved or otherwise known to be true? Clarke, I suspect, viewed it as a necessary truth, intuitively certain, and, hence, not in need of demonstration. But he also may have regarded it as demonstrable. For, as we noted earlier, he appears to hold that the proposition "Something has been produced by nothing" is contradictory. And, if he were right about that, PSR could be demonstrated as follows:

1. *If something exists without a cause then it has been caused by nothing.*
2. *The proposition "Something has been caused by nothing" is contradictory.*

Therefore:

3. *Whatever exists has a cause.*[3]

[3] For reasons of simplicity I have here used the sentence "Whatever exists has a cause" to express the strong version of the Prin-

But, for reasons noted earlier, Clarke provides no good reasons for premise (2) of this argument. Hence, we are justified in rejecting this argument as a *proof* of its conclusion.

According to Hume, Clarke tried to establish that everything that comes into existence must have a cause (the weak version of PSR) by arguing that if something that came into existence did not have a cause it would have to produce itself. But nothing can produce itself, for it would have to exist before it existed in order to

---

ciple of Sufficient Reason. If we were to reject the idea of something's being its own cause, since it would have to bring itself into existence, it is clear that the proposition "Whatever exists has a cause" would not be equivalent to the proposition "Whatever exists exists by reason of the necessity of its own nature or by reason of the causal efficacy of some other being." But there is no need to reject the idea of something's being the cause of itself, since we may understand the expression "self-caused" to mean what is meant by "has the reason of its existence within its own nature." "To say that something—God, for example—is self-caused, or is the cause of its own existence, does not mean that this being brings itself into existence, which is a perfectly absurd idea. Nothing can *bring* itself into existence. To say that something is self-caused (*causa sui*) means only that it exists, not contingently or in dependence upon something else, but by its own nature, which is only to say that it is a being which is such that it can neither come into being nor perish. Now whether such a being in fact exists or not, there is in any case no absurdity in the idea."—Richard Taylor, *Metaphysics* (Englewood Cliffs, N.J.: Prentice-Hall, Inc., 1963), p. 93. Clarke holds a similar view. "Now to be self-existent, is not, to be produced by itself; for that is an express contradiction. But it is, (which is the only idea we can frame of self-existence; and without which, the word seems to have no signification at all:) It is, I say, to exist by an absolute necessity originally in the nature of the thing itself" (*Demonstration*, p. 15).

bring itself into existence—an obvious impossibility.[4] Hume's reply to this argument is certainly correct.

> But this reasoning is plainly inconclusive, because it supposes that in our denial of a cause we still grant what we expressly deny, *viz.*, that there must be a cause, which therefore is taken to be the object itself; and *that*, no doubt, is an evident contradiction. . . . An object that exists absolutely without any cause certainly is not its own cause, and when you assert that the one follows from the other, you suppose the very point in question. . . .[5]
>
> [5] *Ibid.*

One other attempt to demonstrate PSR may be noted. (Hume attributes this argument to Locke.)

> *1. If something exists without a cause, it is caused by nothing.*
>
> *2. Nothing cannot be the cause of something.*
>
> *Therefore:*
>
> *3. Whatever exists must have a cause.*

Hume claims that this argument contains essentially the same mistake as the last.

> It is sufficient only to observe that when we exclude all causes we really do exclude them, and neither suppose nothing nor the object itself to be the causes of the existence, and consequently can draw no argument from the absurdity of these suppositions to prove the absurdity of that exclusion. If everything must have a cause, it follows that upon the exclusion of other causes

[4] *A Treatise of Human Nature*, Book I, Part III, Section III.

we must accept of the object itself or of nothing as causes. But it is the very point in question whether everything must have a cause or not, and therefore, according to all just reasoning, it ought never to be taken for granted.[6]

It is clear from Hume's comment that he rejects premise (1). He takes the proponent of the argument to mean by premise (1) that if something exists without a cause, it nevertheless has a cause—although in this case its cause will not be some other thing, it will be *nothing*. But there is a subtlety in this argument that Hume overlooks, perhaps because it is not present in the previous argument attributed by Hume to Clarke. In the natural sense of the expression "caused by nothing" it is *true* that if something exists without a cause it is caused by nothing—to be caused by nothing is simply not to be caused by any thing whatever. Taken in this way, premise (1) is true. Moreover, premise (2) is true as well. For to say that nothing cannot be the cause of something is simply to say that if something has a cause then there must be some *thing* that is its cause. But so interpreted, the premises, although true, do not yield the conclusion that everything has a cause. For from (1), if something exists without a cause then there is no thing that caused it, and (2), if something has a cause then there is a thing that caused it, it in no way follows that everything has a cause. Therefore, if the premises are interpreted so as to be clearly true, the argument is invalid; whereas, if the argument is to appear valid, its first premise, as Hume points out, is false or, at the very least, begs the question at issue. In either case, the argument fails as a demonstration of **PSR**.

[6] *Ibid.*

Of course, if, as seems likely, PSR cannot be—at least, has not been—demonstrated, it does not follow that it cannot be *known* to be true. Clearly, if we know any propositions to be true, there must be some propositions that we can know to be true without having to *prove* them, without having to derive them from other propositions we know to be true. If this were not so, we would have to know an infinite number of propositions in order to know any proposition whatever.[7] Hence, the fact, if it is a fact, that PSR cannot be demonstrated does not invalidate the view Clarke seems to take— namely, that PSR is a necessary truth, intuitively certain.[8]

Since PSR in its strong form is essential to Clarke's version of the Cosmological Argument, it is important to consider the view that the principle is a necessary truth, known by intuition. However, to consider this matter with some degree of clarity, it is necessary to indicate the sense in which I intend to use a number of technical, philosophical terms. Although, not all the terms I shall discuss here are crucial to an examination of Clarke's view of PSR, they will be needed in discussing later stages of his argument. For convenience, I shall introduce and characterize all these terms now. The main technical, philosophical concepts I need to clarify are: *logically true, logically false, analytically true, analytically false, synthetic, impossible, possible, necessary, contingent, a priori,* and *a posteriori.*

[7] See G. E. Moore, *Some Main Problems of Philosophy* (New York: Humanities Press Inc., 1953), pp. 122-123.

[8] There is, of course, no inconsistency in holding that one and the same proposition is both intuitively and demonstratively certain. A proposition that is known in one way (immediately) may

Perhaps the best procedure for introducing the notion of a logical truth is the one suggested by Quine. Quine lists a number of words that he calls *logical words*: "is," "not," "and," "or," "if," "then," "some," "all," etc.[9] Next, he distinguishes between a word's occurring essentially and vacuously in a sentence. A word occurs essentially in a sentence provided that its replacement in every one of its occurrences by some other word will change the truth-value of the sentence. Thus "lions" in the true statement "There are lions in Africa" occurs essentially since its replacement by the word "tigers" yields the false statement "There are tigers in Africa." A word occurs vacuously in a sentence just in case it does not occur essentially. Armed with the notion of an *essential occurrence* of a word in a sentence, we may introduce the concepts of logically true and logically false as follows:[10]

> *Df. 1: The proposition P, expressed by the sentence S, is* logically true = *df. (i) P is true, and (ii) only logical words occur essentially in S.*

---

also be known mediately, that is, known as the conclusion of an argument whose premises are known to be true.

[9] W. V. Quine, *Mathematical Logic* (New York: Harper Torchbook Edition, 1962), p. 1.

[10] Almost all of the definitions that follow were given to me by Professor George Nakhnikian. However, for simplicity of presentation I have left out some important qualifications. Several of these definitions—presented in terms of sentences rather than propositions—together with the important qualifications may be found in Nakhnikian's *Introduction to Philosophy* (New York: Alfred A. Knopf, 1967), pp. 179-183.

Thus the proposition expressed by the sentence "If every man is mortal and Socrates is a man, then Socrates is mortal" is logically true since the only words occurring essentially in the sentence are logical words. The non-logical words "man," "mortal," "Socrates," occur vacuously.

> Df. 2: *The proposition P, expressed by the sentence S, is* logically false = *df. (i) P is false, and (ii) only logical words occur essentially in S.*

Although the distinction between *analytic* and *synthetic* has been questioned, I shall assume here that there is a distinction to be drawn and that it is not circular to make use of some such term as *synonymous* or *definition* in order to draw the distinction. Accordingly, *analytically true* may be defined as follows:

> Df. 3: *The proposition P, expressed by the sentence S, is* analytically true = *df. P is logically true or S is reducible to S' by means of a definition and S' expresses a proposition P' which is logically true.*

Thus the proposition expressed by the sentence "All brothers are male" is *analytically true* because even though the sentence does not express a logical truth—if "brothers" (a non-logical word) were replaced by "humans," the resulting sentence would express a false proposition—the sentence is reducible by means of a definition to one that does express a logical truth. By the definition of "brother," we may reduce the sentence in question to the sentence "All male siblings are male," in which only logical words occur essentially.

Df. 4: The proposition P, expressed by the sentence S, is analytically false = *df. P is logically false or S is reducible to S' by means of a definition and S' expresses a proposition P' which is logically false.*

For example, the proposition "Some brothers are not male" is analytically false, not logically false.

Df. 5: The proposition P, expressed by the sentence S, is synthetic = *df. P is neither analytically true nor analytically false.*

The modal terms *impossible, possible, necessary* and *contingent* are employed here in the following way. I treat "impossible" as a *primitive* term and define the other modal concepts in terms of it. But some explanation of the notion of "impossible" as it is here used can be given by contrasting it with certain other uses of the term and by providing some examples.

Two uses of "impossible" that are not at issue here are the *causal* use and the *epistemic* use. We use "impossible" on occasions to indicate what is or is not compatible with certain causal truths. Thus I may say "It's impossible for dogs to climb trees but not impossible for cats to do so" or "It is impossible that a man will one day live on the sun but not impossible that he will one day live on the moon." We also use "impossible" to indicate something about the state of our knowledge (the epistemic use). Thus I may say "It's impossible that Jones committed the murder" meaning that I know that he did not. But the use of "impossible" that is important here is neither causal nor epistemic. In the use at issue here, it is not impossible that dogs climb trees and that Jones committed the murder. Philosophers have called this use of "impossible" *logical* or *conceptual* impossibility in contrast to *causal* and *epistemic* impossibility.[11]

Consider the two statements: "It is impossible for me to fly by flapping my arms," and "It is impossible for me to make something both round and square." The task of flying by flapping my arms is certainly an impossible task for me to accomplish. But the impossibility in this case is not logical (conceptual) impossibility. For there are conceivable changes in the universe such that should they have occurred it would not be impossible for me to fly by flapping my arms. For example, suppose my arms had grown to resemble large, powerful wings. In general, when a state of affairs is impossible *but* there are conceivable changes in the universe such that, were they to have occurred, the state of affairs would be possible, the impossibility in question is not logical impossibility. The task of making an object both round and square, however, is a task which I could not do under *any* conceivable circumstances. Hence, the impossibility of accomplishing this task is logical or conceptual.

Although the modal terms may be applied (as I have just done) to tasks and states of affairs, in the following definitions they are applied to propositions. Using "impossible" as our primitive term, we may define the other modal concepts as follows:

Df. 6: P is possible = *df. It is not impossible that P.*

Df. 7: P is necessary = *df. It is impossible that not P.*

---

[11] See, for example, G. E. Moore, *Commonplace Book, 1919-1953* (New York: The Macmillan Company, 1962), pp. 184-188.

81

Df. 8: P is contingent = *df. It is possible that P and it is possible that not P.*

Having introduced these modal terms, we may note a few examples of their application. It is possible that George Washington was not the first President of the United States, but it is impossible that George Washington both was and was not the first President of the United States. It is impossible that some brothers are not male, and it is necessary that if Jones is a brother then he is male. The proposition "George Washington was not the first President of the United States" is a contingent proposition, since both it and its denial are possible. In general, we may observe that every analytically true proposition is necessary and every analytically false proposition is impossible. Also, every contingent proposition is synthetic.[12]

The last two concepts we need are the epistemic concepts: *a priori* and *a posterori.*

Df. 9: P is a priori = *df. The truth value of P can be known without empirical evidence, by just reflecting on and understanding P.*

For example, the proposition "Some brothers are not male" is known *a priori* since once we understand the concepts involved in the proposition we are able to know that it is false—indeed, necessarily false. However, the proposition "There are tigers in India" is one whose

[12] It is an issue of considerable philosophical dispute as to whether all synthetic propositions are contingent. For a brief discussion of this question see Roderick M. Chisholm, *Theory of Knowledge* (Englewood Cliffs, N.J.: Prentice-Hall, Inc., 1966), pp. 87-90.

truth value cannot be known independently of observation and experience. It is known *a posterori*.

> *Df. 10: P is* a posterori = *df. The truth value of P can be known only by means of experience and empirical evidence.*

In terms of the concepts introduced above, I suggest that we understand the view that PSR in its strong form is both necessarily true and intuitively certain as the view that the principle is both *necessary* in the sense defined above and known *a priori*. Assuming that this is Clarke's view, we may now consider what can be said for it and what can be said against it.

If PSR in its strong form is analytically true, then the view we are considering is probably correct. For every analytically true proposition is necessary and, if known at all, presumably can be known by simply reflecting on it, without relying on empirical evidence. But is PSR analytically true? Clearly, the principle is not logically true. Nor, it would seem, does the mere notion of the existence of a thing *definitionally* contain the notion of a thing being caused. Kant argued, correctly I think, that although the proposition "Every effect has a cause" is analytically true, "Every event has a cause" is not. The idea of an event, of something happening—a leaf falling, a chair collapsing—does not seem to contain the idea of something *causing* that event. If this is so, then PSR is not analytically true.

Clarke's view is that the principle is necessary. This is clear from the following response he made in corresponding with a critic:

> Nothing can be more absurd, than to suppose that anything (or any circumstance of any thing) is; and yet that

there be absolutely no reason why it is, rather than not. 'Tis easy to conceive, that we may indeed be utterly ignorant of the reasons, or grounds, or causes of many things. But, that anything is; and that there is a real reason in nature why it is, rather than not; these two are as necessarily and essentially connected, as any two correlates whatever, as height and depth, etc.[13]

But if PSR is not analytically true, how can it be necessary? Indeed, can any proposition be necessary if it is not analytically true? Many philosophers have held that only analytically true propositions are necessary. But it is, I think, reasonable to argue, as some philosophers have, that, for example, the proposition "Whatever is red is colored" is necessary but not analytically true.[14] For (i) we do not seem to have a *definition* of "red" or "colored" in terms of which the sentence "Whatever is red is colored" can be reduced to a sentence expressing a logical truth, and yet (ii) it certainly

[13] The letter from which this passage comes is contained in the work of Clarke's from which our quotations from the *Demonstration* have been taken, p. 490. Clarke's use of the term "reason" is not, I think, to be confused with the notion of purpose. He is not maintaining here that whatever exists must have a purpose of its existence. Rather, he is maintaining that for every existing thing there must be some *explanation* of why it exists rather than not. Such an explanation may *include* purpose, but it cannot be given solely in terms of purpose. Thus if we ask why a certain statue exists rather than not, it will not do to say simply that it exists for the purpose of satisfying aesthetic desires. But Clarke would, I think count the fact that Jones made the statue as an explanation of its existence. And it would still be an explanation if one said, "Jones made the statue for the purpose of satisfying aesthetic desires."

[14] See Chisholm, *Theory of Knowledge*, pp. 87-90.

is *impossible* that something be red and not colored. Thus the proposition "Whatever is red is colored" may well be a synthetic, necessary proposition. Moreover, as Chisholm has argued, there seem to be reasons for the view that the proposition "Necessarily, whatever is red is colored" is known *a priori*. But even if this is correct, as I am inclined to think it is, it is far from clear that PSR is a synthetic, necessary proposition known *a priori*.

The difficulty with the view that the principle, in either its strong or weak form, is *necessary* is that we do seem able to conceive of things existing, or even of things coming into existence, without having to conceive of those things as having an explanation or cause. Unlike the proposition "Some red things are not colored," it does seem conceptually possible that something exists that has no cause or explanation of its existence. As Hume remarks, "The separation, therefore, of the idea of a cause from that of a beginning of existence is plainly possible for the imagination, and consequently the actual separation of those objects is so far possible that it implies no contradiction nor absurdity, . . ."[15] Indeed, not only does the denial of the principle seem to be possible, but philosophers have held that the denial of the principle is *true*.

> . . . many philosophers have maintained that it is not true that everything that exists, or even that everything that has a beginning, has a cause, that is to say, is an effect. The world, they say, contains "spontaneous," free, or uncaused and unoriginated events. In any case

[15] *Treatise*, Book I, Part III, Section III. Also see Thomas Reid's critique of Hume in *Essays on the Intellectual Powers of Man*, Essay VI, Chapter VI.

they assert very positively that there is no way of proving that such uncaused events do not occur.[16]

In view of this and other difficulties, some contemporary defenders of the Cosmological Argument have retreated from the view that PSR is a synthetic, necessary proposition known *a priori*. Instead, they have adopted the somewhat more modest view that the principle is a *metaphysical assumption*, a presupposition we are forced to make in order to make sense of our world. Thus, for example, Copleston, in his B.B.C. debate with Russell, argued that something like PSR is presupposed by science. "I cannot see how science could be conducted on any other assumption than that of order and intelligibility in nature."[17] Of the scientist he says:

> When he experiments to find out some particular truth, behind that experiment lies the assumption that the universe is not simply discontinuous. There is the possibility of finding out a truth by experiment. The experiment may be a bad one, it may lead to no result, or not to the result that he wants, but that at any rate there is the possibility, through experiment, of finding out the truth that he assumes. And that seems to me to assume an ordered and intelligible universe.[18]

[16] John Laird, *Theism and Cosmology* (New York: Philosophical Library, 1942), p. 95.

[17] "The Existence of God, A Debate between Bertrand Russell and Father F. C. Copleston," originally broadcast by the British Broadcasting Corporation in 1948. The debate is reprinted in John Hick, ed., *The Existence of God* (New York: The Macmillan Company, 1964). References are to the debate as reprinted in *The Existence of God*.

[18] *Ibid.*, p. 177.

Another contemporary writer has expressed this view as follows:

> The principle of sufficient reason can be illustrated in various ways, as we have done, and if one thinks about it, he is apt to find that he presupposes it in his thinking about reality, but it cannot be proved. It does not appear to be itself a necessary truth, and at the same time it would be most odd to say it is contingent. If one were to try proving it, he would sooner or later have to appeal to considerations that are less plausible than the principle itself. Indeed, it is hard to see how one could even make an argument for it, without already assuming it. For this reason it might properly be called a presupposition of reason itself. One can deny that it is true, without embarrassment or fear of refutation, but one is apt to find that what he is denying is not really what the principle asserts. We shall, then, treat it here as a datum—not something that is provably true, but as something which all men, whether they ever reflect upon it or not, seem more or less to presuppose.[19]

What are we to make of this view? It must be admitted that it is a good deal more plausible than the view I have ascribed to Clarke: namely, that PSR is a necessary truth, known *a priori*. For the proponent of this more modest view is not contending—or, at least, need not contend—that the principle states a necessary truth about reality. All he contends is that the principle is presupposed by us in our dealings with the world. To this he may add that without this presupposition we cannot make any sense of the world. There are, how-

[19] Taylor, *Metaphysics*, pp. 86-87.

ever, several critical points pertinent to this view that need discussion.

First, does the scientist in his work really assume that everything that happens has a cause? In the debate between Russell and Copleston, Russell took the view that physicists need not and do not assume that every event has a cause. "As for things not having a cause, the physicists assure us that individual quantum transition in atoms have no cause."[20] Again, he remarks:

> . . . a physicist looks for causes; that does not necessarily imply that there are causes everywhere. A man may look for gold without assuming that there is gold everywhere; if he finds gold, well and good, if he doesn't he's had bad luck. The same is true when the physicists look for causes.[21]

How are we to settle this matter? Philosophers who hold that the causal principle is a fundamental assumption reply that the Heisenberg uncertainty principle "tells us something about the success (or lack of it) of the present atomic theory in correlating observations, but not about nature in itself, . . ."[22] Moreover, it is observed that the failure to find causes does not lead anyone to abandon the causal principle. Indeed, it is sometimes argued that it is *impossible* to obtain empirical evidence against the principle.[23] If we do not find

---

[20] "A Debate," p. 176.   [21] *Ibid.*, p. 177.
[22] Father Copleston, "A Debate," p. 176.
[23] G. J. Warnock has argued this in "Every Event Has a Cause," *Logic and Language II*, edited by Antony Flew (London: Blackwell, 1953). Warnock argued that it is impossible to describe any circumstance that could show "Every event has a cause" to be *false*. From the impossibility of falsifying "Every event has a cause," Warnock *inferred* that far from being a necessary truth about nature, the principle is "vacuous and utterly uninforma-

gold in a hill after a careful search, we conclude that there is no gold there to be found. But if we do not find the cause of a certain event, we do not conclude that the event has no cause, only that it is extremely difficult to discover. Perhaps, then, there is some reason to think that we do assume that whatever happens has an explanation or cause.

But even if it is granted that, in our dealings with the world, we presuppose that whatever happens has a cause, there seems to be a serious difficulty confronting the recent defenders of the Cosmological Argument. For what the Cosmological Argument requires—or, more exactly, what the versions argued by Clarke, Copleston, and Taylor require—is what I have called the strong form of PSR. That is, their arguments require as a premise the principle that whatever exists—even an eternal being—has a cause or explanation of its existence. But what we have just granted to be presupposed by us in our dealing with the world is the principle that whatever *happens* has a cause. This latter principle

---

tive." But it is, I think, doubtful that this inference is correct. We must distinguish between (i) being able to specify what would have to happen in nature for "Every event has a cause" to be rendered false, and (ii) being able to *determine* that what would falsify "Every event has a cause" has occurred in nature. What Warnock's argument, if correct, establishes is that we lack the ability described in (ii). (See pp. 106-107 of his article.) But he fails to establish that we lack the ability described in (i). And if we have the ability described in (i) then it would seem that "Every event has a cause" is not vacuous and utterly uninformative. In short, apart from appealing to some form of the Positivist's verification principle of meaning, what Warnock establishes does not suffice for the derivation of his claim that the principle "Every event has a cause" is not a proposition providing information about nature.

implies that whatever begins to exist has a cause, since the coming into existence of a thing is an event, a happening. Thus, the principle we have granted to be presupposed in science and common-sense implies what I have called the weak form of PSR. But it does not imply the strong form of that principle; it does not imply that whatever exists has a cause. If something comes into existence, its coming into existence is something that happens. But if something exists from eternity, its eternal existence is not one of the things that happen. Hence, even if it be granted that we presuppose a cause for whatever *happens*, it does not follow that we presuppose a cause or explanation for whatever *exists*.[24]

Can it reasonably be argued that the strong form of PSR is, as Taylor suggests, a presupposition that all men make, a presupposition of reason itself? We have granted as a presupposition of reason that there must be a cause or explanation for any thing that comes into existence.[25] Thus if we imagine a star to have come into

[24] The important point here is not my claim that the eternal existence of a thing is not an event or a happening. For even if we counted the eternal existence of a thing as a happening, we should still wish, I think, to distinguish the assumption that those happenings consisting in *the coming into existence* of a thing require an explanation from the assumption that those happenings consisting in *the eternal existence* of a thing require an explanation. My point here is (i) that these two assumptions are substantially different, and (ii) that, from the mere fact that we commonly presuppose that events have causes, we cannot legitimately infer that we presuppose both of these assumptions. Perhaps we do. But then again perhaps all we presuppose is that those events consisting in the coming into existence of a thing require an explanation.

[25] Clarke, perhaps for reasons of simplicity, usually speaks of requiring a cause only for the existence of a thing. But, of course, the Principle of Sufficient Reason is not meant to require an

existence, say, a thousand years ago, it is presupposed that there must be an explanation for its having come into existence. That is, it is assumed by us that there must be a set of prior events that was sufficient to cause the birth of that star. To say "Nothing caused the birth of the star, it just popped into existence and there is no reason why it came into existence" is, we have granted, to deny a fundamental presupposition of reason itself. But imagine that there is a star in the heavens that never came into existence, a star that has always existed, that has existed from eternity. Do we presuppose that there must be an explanation for the eternal existence of this star? I am doubtful that we do. But short of a metaphysical investigation of mind and its relation to nature, it seems quite impossible to answer this question. Perhaps, then, our most fruitful course here is simply to note the consequences for the Cosmological Argument of both an affirmative and a negative answer to the following question: Is PSR in its strong form a presupposition of reason itself?

Before considering this last question, however, it is important to clarify the nature of the question concerning a thing's existence to which PSR demands there be an answer. Of the star that came into existence a thou-

---

explanation only for the existence of a thing. Thus if a table is made by a carpenter and subsequently painted red, sawed in half, or even destroyed, Clarke's view—and the view of others who have appealed to the Principle of Sufficient Reason—is that there *must* be an explanation not only for the fact that the table came into existence but also for any change that occurs to it. Thus Clarke remarks (in a passage quoted earlier), "Nothing can be more absurd, than to suppose that any thing (or any circumstance of any thing) is; and yet that there be absolutely *no reason why* it *is*, rather than *not*."

sand years ago, we may ask "Where did it come from?" "What brought it into existence?" or "Why did it come into existence?" Clearly, none of these questions can be asked properly of a star that has existed from eternity. Once we learn that it has always existed, we realize that it never came into existence. But there is a simpler question that can be asked both about the eternally existing star and about the star that came into existence a thousand years ago—namely, "Why does this thing exist?" Although we may answer—or, at least, show to be improper—the question "Why did this thing come into existence?" by pointing out that it has always existed, the question "Why does this thing exist rather than not?" cannot be answered or even turned aside by pointing out that it has always existed. As Taylor has noted:

> . . . it is no answer to the question, why a thing exists, to state *how long* it has existed. A geologist does not suppose that he has explained why there should be rivers and mountains merely by pointing out that they are old. Similarly, if one were to ask, concerning the ball of which we have spoken, for some sufficient reason for its being, he would not receive any answer upon being told that it has been there since yesterday. Nor would it be any better answer to say that it had existed since before anyone could remember, or even that it had always existed; for the question was not one concerning its age but its existence.[26]

The question, then, to which PSR requires an answer is: "Why does this thing exist?" This question, I am claiming, may be sensibly asked about a star that has existed from eternity or one that has existed for only a thousand years. (Whether it can be asked sensibly about

[26] Taylor, *Metaphysics*, p. 88.

the entire universe is an important, controversial issue—
an issue that will be discussed when we consider Clarke's
arguments for Proposition II.)

It should be clear that it is one thing to argue, as I
have done, that the question "Why does this thing
exist?" makes sense when asked of something that has
always existed and another thing to argue, as I have
not done, that all men presuppose that there must be
an adequate answer to that question, even when it is
asked about something that has existed from eternity.
We have granted as a presupposition of reason that there
must be an adequate answer to the question when the
being of which it is asked has come into existence. But,
as I have indicated, it seems at least doubtful that the
strong form of PSR is a presupposition of reason itself.

Suppose, as Taylor, Copleston, and others have
claimed, that PSR in its strong form is a metaphysical
assumption that all men make, whether or not they
reflect sufficiently to become aware of the assumption.
What bearing would this have on the Cosmological
Argument? It would not, of course, show that it is a
good argument. For (1) the argument could be invalid,
(2) some premise other than the premise expressing the
principle could be false, and (3) even the premise expressing the principle could be false. The fact, if it is a
fact, that all of us presuppose that whatever exists has
an explanation of its existence does not imply that nothing exists without a reason for its existence. Nature is
not bound to satisfy our presuppositions. As James has
remarked in another connection, "In the great board-
ing-house of nature, the cakes and the butter and the
syrup seldom come out so even and leave the plates so
clean." However, if we do make such a presupposition,
we could not *consistently* reject the Cosmological Argu-

ment solely because it contains PSR as a premise. That is, if we reject the argument, it must be for some reason other than its appeal to PSR.

What we have seen thus far is (i) that it is doubtful that the strong form of PSR is a presupposition we make in dealing with our world, (ii) that even if PSR is a presupposition of reason it does not follow that PSR is known to be true or that it is even true, (iii) that PSR does not appear to be analytically true, and (iv) that PSR does not appear to be a synthetic, necessary truth, known *a priori*. From (iii) and (iv), we can reasonably infer that the Cosmological Argument—insofar as it requires the strong form of PSR as a premise—cannot be a *proof* of the existence of God. For unless there is a way of knowing the principle to be true other than those we have explored, it follows that we do not know the principle to be true. But if we do not know that one of the essential premises of an argument is true then we do not know that it is a good argument for its conclusion. It may, of course, be a perfectly good argument. But if to claim of an argument that it is a *proof* of its conclusion is to imply that its premises are *known* to be true, then we are not entitled to claim that the Cosmological Argument is a proof of the existence of God.

Allowing that PSR may be true, I have argued that it cannot be used as a premise in an argument that is to be a proof of its conclusion. For an argument constitutes a proof of its conclusion only if its premises are known to be true; and, as I have argued above, we do not know that PSR is true. But perhaps in allowing that PSR may (i.e., for all we know) be true, we are allowing too much. Many philosophers take the view that PSR is demonstrably false. It is, of course, important to examine their arguments, for, if their arguments are successful, the Cosmological Argument is unsound (since one of its essential premises is shown to be false).

It follows, it is sometimes argued, from the nature of explanation that PSR is false. Flew develops this argument as follows:

> At every stage explanation is in terms of something else which, at that stage, has to be accepted as a brute fact. In some further stage that fact itself may be explained; but still in terms of something else which, at least temporarily, has simply to be accepted (Hospers). It would therefore seem to be a consequence of the essential nature of explanation that, however much may ultimately be explained in successive stages of inquiry, there must always be some facts which have simply to be accepted with what Samuel Alexander used to call "natural piety" . . . . The ultimate facts about God would have to be, for precisely the same reason, equally inexplicable. In each and every case we must necessarily find at the end of every explanatory road some ultimates which have simply to be accepted as the fundamental truths about the way things are. And this itself is a contention, not about the lamentable contingent facts of the human condition, but about what follows necessarily from the nature of explanation.[27]

PSR in its strong form says that whatever exists has an explanation of its existence. If the argument presented by Flew is a demonstration of the falsity of the principle, it must be a demonstration of the principle's denial (or some statement that entails the principle's denial): namely, that some thing or fact has no explana-

[27] Antony Flew, *God and Philosophy* (London: Hutchinson, 1966), p. 83.

tion of its existence. It is, I think, clear that Flew's argument does not yield the conclusion that some fact has no explanation. The conclusion it yields is that there is always some fact or other that must be left unexplained by us. But this is compatible with every fact's having an explanation. From the premise that we cannot explain every fact, it simply does not follow that there is some fact that cannot be explained.

Although the premises of Flew's argument are not inconsistent with PSR, they do have serious implications for the Cosmological Argument. The point of the Cosmological Argument is to show that there must be a stopping place to the series of explanations. The argument seeks to establish that there must be some ultimate being that is the explanation of other beings, but does not have the explanation of its existence in any other being. Granting this for the moment, it follows from Flew's premises that the existence of this being will be ultimate, but *unexplained*. It will be unexplained because one of Flew's premises is that "at every stage explanation is in terms of something else." But if nothing else can be the explanation of this ultimate being, and if *any* explanation of its existence would have to be in terms of something else, it follows that the existence of this ultimate being is an inexplicable brute fact. However, PSR requires an explanation for the existence of absolutely every being. Hence, although Flew's premises are consistent with PSR, they are inconsistent with the principle when they are conjoined with what, in part, the Cosmological Argument seeks to establish: namely, that there is a being whose existence is not explainable in terms of anything else.

What is puzzling about Flew's remarks is why he should think that it follows from the nature of explanation that "at every stage explanation is in terms of something else." He does provide a few examples in which we do explain one thing in terms of something else—explaining why "the new white paint above our gas cooker quickly turns a dirty brown," etc. But these examples, of course, in no way show that explanation *must* always be in terms of something else. Indeed, even if every generally accepted explanation that has been given is an explanation of one thing in terms of something else, it hardly follows that the nature of explanation requires that it be so. Clarke, Leibniz, and other philosophers who have employed PSR in the Cosmological Argument contend that, in the case of the ultimate being, the explanation of its existence is to be found not in some other being but in its own nature. That the nature of explanation renders this contention impossible needs to be established by a careful analysis of the concept of explanation. Merely citing a few examples in which the explanation of one thing is found in something else is simply irrelevant to the question at issue. Hence, although the principle may be false, Flew's argument fails as a demonstration of its falsity.

Although Flew's argument fails, there is another argument against PSR that demands serious consideration. I shall examine this argument in some detail. Before doing so, however, we need to consider the full implications of PSR.

In our statements of the Cosmological Argument we employed the premise "Whatever exists has a reason for its existence either in the necessity of its own nature or in the causal efficacy of some other being." I identified this premise with PSR. But if we reflect for a moment, it will be apparent that this premise is not identical with PSR—at least as PSR was understood by Leibniz and Clarke. For this premise implies *only* that every existing thing has a reason for its existence. Thus if we come upon a man in a room, our premise implies that there must be a reason why that particular man exists. But, as stated, our premise doesn't imply that there must be a reason why the man in question is in the room he is in, rather than somewhere else. As stated, our premise does not imply that there must be a reason why the man in question is in poor health, say, or a reason why he is at the moment thinking of Paris rather than, say, Lafayette, Indiana. But surely PSR is meant to imply that there must be a reason not only for the existence of the man in question but also for the fact that he is in a particular room at a certain time, in poor health, and thinking of Paris. That is, PSR is taken to imply that there must be not only an explanation of the existence of any object *x* but also an explanation of the possession by *x* of any of its properties. Leibniz's statements of PSR make this clear.

> Nothing happens without a reason why it should be so, rather than otherwise.[28]

> The principle in question is the principle of the want of a sufficient reason in order to anything's existing, in order to any event's happening, in order to any truth's taking place.[29]

Clarke, too, appears to understand PSR as requiring a reason not only for the fact than an object *x* exists but for *any fact* about *x*. Thus (as I noted earlier in a foot-

---

[28] *The Leibniz-Clarke Correspondence*, edited with an introduction by H. G. Alexander (Manchester: Manchester University Press, 1956), 2nd Letter.
[29] *Ibid.*, 5th Letter.

note) he says: "Nothing can be more absurd than to suppose that any thing (or any *circumstance* of any thing) is; and yet that there be absolutely no reason why it is, rather than not" [italics mine].

PSR, then, appears to imply (i) that for any existing object x there is a reason why x exists, and (ii) that for any property P possessed by x there is a reason why x has P. Sometimes, according to Leibniz and Clarke, the reason is to be found within x itself. Thus in the case of the existence of God and His possession of certain essential attributes (power, wisdom, goodness, etc.) both Leibniz and Clarke maintain that these states of affairs contain their own explanations. The statements expressing these states of affairs ("God exists," "God is good," etc.) are, according to Leibniz and Clarke, *necessarily* true. And the states of affairs recorded by these statements are *necessary*. Other states of affairs (i.e., the existence of various objects and their possession of various properties) and the statements that record them are, according to Leibniz and Clarke, *contingent*, they might not have been. These contingent states of affairs are explained by other states of affairs; they are not self-explanatory. Thus the state of affairs constituted by a certain table's being red is contingent and has its explanation in some other state of affairs.

We can now develop the argument against PSR mentioned above. The basic structure of the argument may be exhibited as follows:

1. *PSR implies that every state of affairs has a reason either within itself or in some other state of affairs.*
2. *There are contingent states of affairs.*

3. *If there are contingent states of affairs then there is some state of affairs for which there is no reason.*

Therefore:

4. *PSR is false.*

The reasoning in support of premise (3) proceeds as follows. Consider the state of affairs S expressed by the proposition "There are contingent states of affairs." Clearly it is a contingent matter that there are contingent states of affairs. Hence, S itself is a contingent state of affairs. There must, then, according to PSR, be some state of affairs that is the reason for S, which accounts for the fact that there are contingent states of affairs rather than not. Suppose someone says that the state of affairs constituted by the existence of God is what accounts for S, giving as his reason that God caused there to be contingent states of affairs. We then ask whether the existence of God is a contingent or a necessary state of affairs. If the existence of God is a contingent state of affairs, it cannot account for S; it cannot explain why there are contingent states of affairs rather than not— no more than citing the existence of Adam and his act of generating children can explain why there are any men rather than none. Hence, the defender of PSR must say that the state of affairs constituted by the existence of God is a *necessary* state of affairs. We then ask whether the state of affairs recorded by the proposition "God caused there to be contingent states of affairs" is a contingent or a necessary state of affairs. If *God's causing there to be contingent states of affairs* is itself a contingent state of affairs then it cannot account for S; it cannot explain why there are contingent states of affairs rather than not. That is, if the question to be answered is "Why are there any contingent states of affairs rather than none?" we cannot answer it by appealing to some contingent state of affairs. Consequently, the defender of PSR must say that *God's causing there to be contingent states of affairs* is itself a necessary state of affairs. But if the existence of God is necessary and God's causing there to be contingent states of affairs is also necessary, it follows that it is *necessary* that there are contingent states of affairs. But as we noted at the outset, it is contingent, not necessary, that there are contingent states of affairs. Hence, there can be no explanation of S; there can be no explanation of the fact that there are contingent states of affairs. Consequently, since PSR implies that there is a reason for S, implies that there is an explanation of the fact that there are contingent states of affairs, PSR is false.

In reply to this argument, one might contend that it rests on the mistaken assumption that it is a *contingent* matter that there are contingent states of affairs. For suppose we say that every *true*, contingent proposition records an *actual*, contingent state of affairs. On this view it will not be a contingent matter that there are actual, contingent states of affairs. Indeed, that some contingent states of affairs are *actual* will be necessarily the case. For consider any contingent proposition p and its denial —p. Let us say that p, if true, records the actual contingent state of affairs *s*; and —p, if true, records the actual, contingent state of affairs *s'*. Now it is necessary that either p is true or —p is true. Consequently, it is necessary that either *s* is actual or *s'* is actual. Hence, it is necessary that some contingent state of affairs is actual. But, if so, then it is not a contingent matter that there are actual, contingent states of affairs— -

no more than it is a contingent matter that some contingent proposition is true. It is impossible that no contingent propositions are true. So it is impossible that no contingent states of affairs are actual. It is necessary, in other words, that there are actual, contingent states of affairs.

So long as we suppose that every *true*, contingent proposition records an *actual* state of affairs, there is no way of avoiding the conclusion that it is *not* a contingent matter that some contingent states of affairs are *actual*. In order to save the argument against PSR, we might adopt the view that only the positive member of a pair of contradictories (p, —p) records, when true, an actual state of affairs. Thus we might claim that the true, positive proposition "There are elephants" records an actual state of affairs, while denying that the true, negative statement "It is not the case that there are centaurs" records an actual state of affairs. That is, we might hold that only true, *positive*, contingent propositions record actual states of affairs. Although such a view avoids postulating negative facts, it creates difficulties for a correspondence theory of truth. For if a proposition is true by virtue of corresponding to some actual state of affairs then, since the proposition "It is not the case that there are centaurs" is true, it would seem that it is so by virtue of corresponding to some actual state of affairs. And the natural thing to suppose is that the state of affairs in question is simply *the non-existence of centaurs*.

It is not my purpose here (nor is it within my competence) to investigate in any detail the metaphysical problems associated with the correspondence theory of truth, negative facts, etc. My aim is to determine whether the argument against PSR is a good argument.

As we have seen, those who hold that *every* true, contingent proposition records an actual state of affairs can (indeed, must) reject the assumption that it is a contingent matter that there are contingent states of affairs. Since that assumption was crucial to the reasoning in support of the third premise of the argument against PSR, it seems that unless we challenge the view that every true, contingent proposition records an actual state of affairs, we must abandon our claim to have found a good argument against PSR—for our reasoning has been shown to rest on the unfounded assumption that it is a contingent matter that there are contingent states of affairs.

In defending the argument against PSR, we need not challenge the view that every true, contingent proposition records an actual state of affairs. For the argument against PSR can be reformulated so as to avoid the assumption that it is a contingent matter that there are contingent states of affairs. Let us introduce the idea of *a positive, contingent state of affairs* as follows: X is a positive, contingent state of affairs if and only if from the fact that X obtains it follows that at least one contingent being exists.[30] That there are elephants, for example, is a positive, contingent state of affairs. For, from the fact that it obtains, it follows that at least one contingent being exists. That there are no unicorns, however, is not a positive, contingent state of affairs. That God knows there are elephants is a positive, contingent state of affairs, and this is so even on the assumption that God is not a contingent being. That God knows there are no unicorns is, however, not a positive, contingent state of affairs if God is not a contingent being.

[30] I am indebted to Alvin Plantinga for this characterization of a positive, contingent state of affairs.

Consider the general state of affairs *t* recorded by the proposition "There are positive, contingent states of affairs." Is *t* itself a contingent or a necessary state of affairs? It is reasonable, I think, to claim that *t* is a contingent state of affairs. For although contingent beings do exist, it does not seem to be necessary that contingent beings exist. I should think that one of Leibniz's possible worlds is a world in which the only beings that exist are necessary beings. Of course, if every true contingent statement records an actual state of affairs, there is no possible world in which only necessary states of affairs obtain. Each possible world contains some contingent states of affairs. But a contingent state of affairs may obtain in a given world—e.g., the state of affairs recorded by the proposition "There are no centaurs"—without it being true that any contingent beings exist in that world. But if, as it seems reasonable to believe, there is a possible world in which no contingent beings exist, then *t* is a contingent state of affairs. For if that world were the actual world, the state of affairs *t* would not obtain—since if *t* did obtain it would follow that some contingent being exists. Unlike S (the state of affairs recorded by the proposition "There are contingent states of affairs"), *t*, it appears, is a contingent state of affairs.

Armed with the idea of a positive, contingent state of affairs, we may now reformulate the argument against PSR as follows:

1. *PSR implies that every state of affairs has an explanation either within itself or in some other state of affairs.*
2. *There are positive, contingent states of affairs.*
3. *If there are positive, contingent states of affairs,*

then there is some state of affairs for which there is no explanation.

Therefore:

4. *PSR is false.*

The reasoning in support of premise (3) proceeds as follows. Consider the general state of affairs *t* recorded by the proposition "There are positive, contingent states of affairs." As we noted above, *t* certainly appears to be a contingent state of affairs. There must, then, according to PSR, be some state of affairs that explains *t*. Suppose that *q* is the state of affairs that explains *t* and that "*q* explains *t*" is made true by the fact that the actual state of affairs *q* stands in a certain relation R to *t*. The actual state of affairs *q*R*t* must entail the state of affairs *t*, otherwise the fact that *q*R*t* would not make it true that *q* explains *t*. But the fact that *t* obtains entails that at least one contingent being exists. Therefore, the actual state of affairs *q*R*t* entails that at least one contingent being exists. Now the actual state of affairs *q*R*t* is either necessary or contingent. It cannot be necessary, for *t* would then be necessary. Consequently, the actual state of affairs *q*R*t* (i) is contingent and (ii) entails that there exists at least one contingent being. This means that the actual state of affairs *q*R*t* is *a positive, contingent state of affairs.* This being so, it is clear that *q*R*t* cannot make it true that *q* explains *t*. For to explain *t*, *q* must explain why there are positive, contingent states of affairs—and clearly *q* cannot serve this explanatory role by virtue of standing in relation R to *t*, if the fact that *q* stands in relation R to *t* is itself a positive, contingent state of affairs. The fact in virtue of which *q* explains why there are positive, contingent states of affairs cannot itself be a positive, contingent state of affairs.

To take an example, suppose we try to explain why there are positive, contingent states of affairs by citing the fact, let us suppose, that God willed that positive, contingent states of affairs be actual—just as, for example, we might explain why there are men by citing the (supposed) fact that God willed that men should exist. The fact, then, consisting of God's willing that positive, contingent states of affairs be actual is what explains why there are positive, contingent states of affairs. But now let us consider the fact of God's willing that positive, contingent states of affairs be actual. If that fact does explain why there are positive, contingent states of affairs it must entail that some positive, contingent states of affairs are actual. And if this is so, then the fact that God willed that there be positive, contingent states of affairs entails that at least one contingent being exists. We then ask whether the fact in question is contingent or necessary. It cannot be necessary, for then it would be necessary that at least one contingent being exists—and, as we have seen, it seems to be a contingent matter that contingent beings exists. What follows, then, is that the fact consisting of God's willing that positive, contingent states of affairs be actual is *itself* a positive, contingent state of affairs; for it is contingent and, from the fact that it obtains, it follows that at least one contingent being exists. But clearly, the fact that *accounts* for why there are positive, contingent states of affairs *cannot* itself be a positive, contingent state of affairs.

I conclude from the above that *t* is an actual state of affairs that cannot be explained and that, therefore, the reformulated argument against PSR is a good argument—it provides, if you like, a sufficient reason for believing that PSR is false.

The argument I have just advanced is not, however, the only argument of its kind that can be given against PSR. James F. Ross has proposed an argument against PSR that proceeds along lines similar to the first argument I presented.[31] However, instead of considering the *general* state of affairs recorded by "There are contingent states of affairs," Ross asks us to consider the state of affairs W, which is constituted by all actual, contingent states of affairs not identical with W itself. The proposition 'W' that expresses W is "the logically complex proposition constituted by the conjunction of every true contingent proposition that is not equivalent to 'W'." Ross then argues that W is a contingent state of affairs, that there is no state of affairs q that explains or accounts for W, and that, therefore, PSR is false. His argument, in brief, is that, if q explains W, then q cannot be contingent; otherwise it would be a part of W, and W (a contingent state of affairs) would be self-accounting, which is impossible. But if q is a necessary state of affairs we must ask whether *q's explaining W* is also necessary. If it is then W would be necessary (which it clearly is not). If *q's explaining W* is contingent, then it is part of W and itself requires explanation—in which case we are led into a vicious infinite regress. Consequently, there can be no explanation for the contingent state of affairs W; and PSR, therefore, is false.[32]

[31] James F. Ross, *Philosophical Theology* (Indianapolis: The Bobbs-Merrill Company, Inc., 1969), pp. 295-304.

[32] There is, I think, a serious difficulty in Ross's argument. The following principle seems true; namely, *if every conjunct of a*

Ross is anxious to employ some principle of explanation in a proof of God's existence. Having rejected PSR, he turns to another principle that he contends is true and does the job (i.e., performs the crucial role in an argument for the existence of God) for which traditional philosophers employed PSR. It will be instructive to consider Ross's principle, since doing so will bring to light a major difference between the argument I have employed against PSR and Ross's own argument.

Ross's principle may be stated as follows: For any actual, contingent state of affairs p it is *logically possible* that there is some actual state of affairs q that explains p. Now it appears at first glance that this principle is refuted by the very argument he employed to refute PSR. For consider W "the one and only state of affairs constituted by every state of affairs expressed by a true contingent statement." "Is there anything to account for W? No, as the earlier arguments made clear: W is unexplained, unaccounted for."[33] Could W be accounted for? Is it logically possible that there be some state of affairs q that accounts for W? Ross argues for an affirmative answer to these questions. It is, of course, necessarily true that the one and only state of affairs constituted by every state of affairs expressed by a true contingent statement is without explanation. But this

---

conjunctive state of affairs is explained then the conjunctive state of affairs is explained. But if this principle is true then if we think of W (as Ross does) as the *mere conjunction* of the particular states of affairs that are actual, then if every one of those states of affairs is explained, W itself will be explained. And if W has an infinite number of conjuncts, each conjunct explained by some other conjunct, then it will be true that every conjunct in W is explained and true, therefore, that W is explained.

33 *Philosophical Theology*, p. 307.

necessity implies only the following with respect to W: It is necessarily true that if W is identical with the one and only state of affairs constituted by every state of affairs expressed by a true contingent statement then W has no explanation. Since W is identical with the one and only state of affairs constituted by every state of affairs expressed by a true contingent statement, it follows that W is unexplained. But for W to refute Ross's principle, it must be *necessary* that W be unexplained. And the latter will be the case only if W is necessarily, not contingently, identical with the one and only state of affairs constituted by every state of affairs expressed by a true contingent statement. But the identity in question is contingent, not necessary. As Ross notes, "that W (the conjunction of what happens to be actual) is what is actually designated by 'W' is itself contingent."[34] Ross concludes that, although W is unexplained, it is not logically impossible for there to have been some state of affairs q that accounts for W. Hence, W does not constitute an exception to his principle of explanation.

I think Ross is correct in claiming that the argument he has used to dispose of PSR does not dispose of his principle of explanation. But I also think that the reformulated argument I have used against PSR does dispose of Ross's principle.

The state of affairs *t* recorded by the statement "There are positive, contingent states of affairs" is, I have argued, unexplained—in this respect it may resemble Ross's W. But, unlike W, it is logically impossible for there to be some state of affairs q that explains *t*. To see that this is so, we must first see that the *general*

[34] "W" is the definite description: "the one and only state of affairs constituted by every state of affairs expressed by a true, contingent statement."

state of affairs t is not identical with the complex state of affairs P constituted by all the actual, *particular*, positive, contingent states of affairs. That it is not can be seen by analogy with other general states of affairs. Consider, for example, the general state of affairs M recorded by the proposition "There are men." Suppose the actual world contained only three men: a, b, and c. Consider the complex state of affairs A that is constituted by the three particular states of affairs: the existence of a, the existence of b, and the existence of c. Now the general state of affairs M is not identical with A. For suppose a possible world containing men (say, d and e), but containing neither a, b, nor c, had been the actual world. A, clearly, would not have been an actual state of affairs; whereas, M would have been actual. Put somewhat differently, M is a constituent both of the actual world containing a, b, and c and of *any* other possible world containing men. But A is a constituent only of those possible worlds containing the particular men a, b, and c. Consequently, the state of affairs A is not identical with the general state of affairs M. Similarly, the state of affairs t is not identical with the state of affairs P. t is a constituent of every possible world that contains any positive, contingent states of affairs. P is a constituent only of those possible worlds containing the particular, positive, contingent states of affairs that are actual in our world.

P, perhaps, is an unexplained state of affairs.[35] But it is logically possible that there be a positive, contingent state of affairs q that explains P. It is logically possible because it is a contingent and not a necessary truth that the positive, contingent states of affairs constituting P are the only actual, particular, positive, contingent

<hr/>

[35] But see note 32.

states of affairs. Hence, P does not provide us with a refutation of Ross's principle.

t (which, as we saw, is not identical with P), however, is such that it is not logically possible for there to be a state of affairs q that explains it. Clearly, no positive, contingent state of affairs can account for the fact that there are positive, contingent states of affairs. Now if, as seems reasonable, we rule out contingent states of affairs that are not positive—i.e., that are such that from the fact that they obtain it does not follow that at least one contingent being exists—as not sufficient to account for the fact that there are positive, contingent states of affairs, we are left with necessary states of affairs; and, as the earlier arguments have shown, it is impossible to explain contingent states of affairs solely by reference to necessary states of affairs. Consequently, I conclude that *t* is such that it is logically impossible for there to be some state of affairs that accounts for it. Ross's principle, therefore, is false.

PSR plays an essential role in the version of the Cosmological Argument we are considering. Earlier I concluded that, since we do not *know* that PSR is true, we are not entitled to claim that the Cosmological Argument is a proof of its conclusion. This does not imply, of course, that the argument is unsound. But in view of our evaluation of the argument against PSR, we now seem to have a much more forceful criticism of the Cosmological Argument. For, since PSR is required as a premise and since we now have adequate grounds for concluding that PSR is false, it appears that we have adequate grounds for concluding that the Cosmological Argument is unsound. It is unsound because one of its premises—namely, PSR—is false.

The difficulty with this rejection of the Cosmological

Argument is that our formulation of the argument does not contain the version of PSR that the reformulated argument shows to be false. The version of PSR that occurs as a premise of the Cosmological Argument, as we observed earlier, concerns only the *existence* of things. It says of each existing thing that it exists either by reason of the necessity of its own nature or by reason of the causal efficacy of some other being. What we have shown to be false (if the reformulated argument is successful) is a much more *general* principle; namely, the principle that every actual state of affairs has a reason either within itself or in some other state of affairs. Since the principle employed in the Cosmological Argument does not entail the more general principle refuted by the reformulated argument against PSR, the defender of the Cosmological Argument, it seems, can safely admit that the more general principle is false without thereby relinquishing his acceptance of the argument.

It can, of course, be argued that the only reason someone would have for accepting the version of PSR that occurs as a premise in the Cosmological Argument is whatever reason he might have for believing the more general principle refuted by the reformulated argument. In support of this view, it can be pointed out that both Leibniz and Clarke hold versions of PSR much more general than the version that appears in the Cosmological Argument. But even if this is so, our refutation of the more general version of PSR would (at best) deprive the defender of the Cosmological Argument of his *grounds* for accepting the restricted version of PSR that appears as a premise in the argument. It would not in the least show that the restricted version is *false*. And it is the latter that needs showing if the critic wishes to justify his view that the Cosmological

Argument is unsound. Consequently, we must conclude that the fact that the more general version of PSR has been shown to be false does not establish that the Cosmological Argument is unsound.

One conclusion that our reflections thus far do yield is that there is no such thing as *the* Principle of Sufficient Reason. There is, it would seem, a variety of logically related principles that might properly be called "versions" of PSR—just as there is a variety of arguments that are properly called "versions" of the Cosmological Argument. If the reformulated argument is a good argument, the most general version of PSR has been shown to be false. Let us call this version of PSR "PSR$_1$." Thus, given the soundness of the reformulated argument, we can say that the following version of PSR is *false*.

> PSR$_1$: *Every actual state of affairs has a reason either within itself or in some other state of affairs.*

The version of PSR that is a premise in the Cosmological Argument we may call "PSR$_2$."

> PSR$_2$: *Every existing thing has a reason for its existence either in the necessity of its own nature or in the causal efficacy of some other being.*

I have said that PSR$_1$ is much more *general* than PSR$_2$ because PSR$_2$ implies only that there must be an explanation of the *existence* of an object x. It does not imply that there must be an explanation of *every* fact about x. Thus if we find a man in a room, PSR$_2$ requires that there be an explanation of the fact that the man exists. It does not require that there be an explanation of the fact that the man is in the particular room he is in. The reformulated argument, if good, establishes that there is at least one state of affairs that has no explanation. Hence, the reformulated argument, if good, establishes that PSR_1 is false. But the reformulated argument does not yield the conclusion that there is some existing thing such that there is no explanation of its *existence*. Hence, the reformulated argument, if good, does not establish that PSR_2 is false. If the Cosmological Argument can make do with PSR_2 then the reformulated argument cannot show that the Cosmological Argument is unsound.

What led us to develop the reformulated argument is not the Cosmological Argument as such, but the fact that the proponents of the argument—particularly Leibniz and Clarke—appear to accept a version of PSR much stronger than PSR_2 (the version of PSR that occurs as a premise in the argument). Indeed, it seems that both Leibniz and Clarke accept something like PSR_1. If they do, then they are mistaken. But so far as the Cosmological Argument is concerned, Clarke, at least, employs as a premise not PSR_1 but PSR_2. And, as I have insisted, it does not follow from his being mistaken in accepting PSR_1 that he is mistaken in accepting PSR_2.[36]

[36] For further consideration of PSR see pp. 146-151 of Chapter III.

III

Two Criticisms of the
Cosmological Argument

THE Cosmological Argument, as I indicated earlier, has two parts. The first part consists of an argument for the existence of a necessary being; the second part consists of an argument for the conclusion that a necessary being must have the properties traditionally ascribed to God. We are here considering the first part of Clarke's version of the argument—that is, we are considering Clarke's argument for the existence of a necessary being. This argument, as we noted earlier, is developed in three steps. The first step is to demonstrate that something has been in existence from eternity (Proposition I).[1] Step two is to demonstrate that "There has existed from eternity some one unchangeable and independent being" (Proposition II).[2]

---

[1] Clarke, as we noted, does not mean by Proposition I that some *one* being has been in existence from eternity. What he means is that there has never been a time when nothing was in existence. Locke had committed the blunder of thinking that from the fact that (i) something exists now, and (ii) nothing cannot produce a real being, it followed that "something must have existed from eternity," meaning that there must be *an eternal being*. (*An Essay Concerning Human Understanding*, Book II, Chapter X) Clarke's argument does not contain this piece of fallacious reasoning.

[2] By the expression "some one" Clarke means "at least one." "The meaning of this proposition, (and all that the argument here requires,) is, that there must needs have always been some

Step three is to demonstrate that "That unchangeable and independent being which has existed from eternity, without any external cause of its existence; must be self-existent, that is necessarily-existing" (Proposition III). In this chapter, I shall discuss Proposition II and the reasons Clarke gives in support of it.

It will, I think, simplify and clarify Clarke's argument if we alter somewhat the conclusion that he endeavors to establish in step two of his argument. From the discussion of the main argument that Clarke gives for Proposition I, it is clear that the fundamental idea in Clarke's Cosmological Argument is the idea of a being for which the ground or reason why it exists rather than not is to be found in the necessity of its own nature. What the strong form of PSR precludes is the possibility that there exists a being for which there is absolutely no reason or explanation why it exists rather than not. Since from eternity something has been in existence and since everything that exists must have an explanation of its existence, Clarke envisages two apparent possibilities. First, it might be that from eternity there has been a succession of beings each having the reason for its existence in the causal efficacy of some other being. That is, it might be that no being has the reason of its existence in the necessity of its own nature. Second, it might be that there exists, and has always existed, at least one being that has the reason of its existence in the necessity of its own nature. Now the point of step two of Clarke's argument is to establish that the first apparent possibility is only apparent, that it is not a possible state of affairs at all. In short, Clarke proposes to establish in

independent being, some one at least. To show that there can be no more than one is not the design of this proposition, but of the seventh" (p. 11).

step two that a being exists for which the ground or reason why it exists rather than not is to be found in the necessity of its own nature. (In step three it is then argued that such a being would be a *necessary being*, a being whose non-existence is impossible.) It will, therefore, be useful here if we develop the argument of step two as an argument for the conclusion that there exists a being that has the reason for its existence within its own nature.[3]

Clarke begins his argument as follows:

> For since something must needs have been from eternity; as has been already proved, and is granted on all hands: either there has always existed some one unchangeable and independent being, from which all other beings that are or ever were in the universe, have received their original; or else there has been an infinite succession of changeable and dependent beings produced one from another in an endless progression, without any original cause at all (*Demonstration*, pp. 11-12).

If we alter this passage in accordance with my suggestion, the inference with which Clarke begins is from

1. Something has existed from eternity.

to

2. Either there exists a being that has the reason of its existence within its own nature or there has been an infinite succession of beings, each having the reason of its existence in the causal efficacy of some other being.

---

[3] This way of developing the argument of step two also has the advantage of fitting in nicely with the way in which Hume has Demea summarize Clarke's argument.

Using the expression "dependent being" to mean "a being that has the reason of its existence in the causal efficacy of some other being," and the expression "independent being" to mean "a being that has the reason of its existence within its own nature," we may express (2) as: either there exists an *independent* being or there has been an infinite succession of *dependent* beings. (Clarke may be using "independent being" to mean simply "any being that exists and requires nothing else for its existence." But, given the strong form of PSR, it still would follow that an independent being *must* have the reason of its existence within its own nature.)

It may be objected that (2) does not follow from (1). For (1) tells us simply that from eternity something or other has been in existence, which would be true even if the only thing that exists now or has ever existed is an infinitely old star for which there is no explanation of why it exists rather than not. But if this were so it would not be true that either an independent being exists or there has been an infinite succession of dependent beings. Or, consider the possibility that from eternity there has been a *finite* succession of beings. That is, suppose that the first member of this succession is a being that never came into existence, but ceased to exist, say, a thousand years ago. Suppose that the second member came into existence some time prior to the demise of the first member and has the first for its cause, and so on up to the present. Clearly no member of this succession is an independent being. The succession consists of a finite number of beings and yet there never was a time when no member of the succession was in existence. But if the universe consisted of such a succession of beings it would be true that from eternity something has been in existence, but false that an independent be-

118

ing exists, and false that there has been an infinite succession of dependent beings. Therefore, it seems clear that the inference from (1) to (2) is invalid.

Clarke, I believe, can be defended against this objection. But to rule out the two possibilities described above, we must have recourse to PSR. The principle requires an explanation for the existence of absolutely every being. But in our first possibility we envisaged the universe to consist of a single, infinitely old star for which there is no reason why it exists rather than not. The existence of such a universe is incompatible with PSR. The second possibility also conflicts with the principle. For if the universe consists of a finite succession of beings, the first member of which never came into existence, there would be no explanation for the existence of the first member. Hence, if, as PSR requires, absolutely every being must have an explanation of its existence, and if (1) something has been in existence from eternity, then it follows that (2) either there is an independent being or there has been an infinite succession of dependent beings.

One might reply that this defense of Clarke does not quite meet the objection. For the objection was that Clarke's inference from (1) to (2) is invalid. All that has been said in defense of Clarke is that (2) follows from (1) *in conjunction with* PSR. It has not been shown that (2) follows from (1) alone. Although this must be admitted, the objection, I think, turns out not to be very significant. For since PSR is already a premise in Clarke's Cosmological Argument, it seems captious not to count it as a suppressed premise in his argument for (2). Moreover, if the principle is, as Clarke claims, a *necessary truth*, then if (2) follows from (1) in conjunction with the principle—as was argued above—it also follows from (1) *alone.* (Any deductively valid argument containing a premise that is a necessary truth will be deductively valid even if the premise that is necessarily true is deleted.)

Before citing the passage in which Clarke endeavors to establish that it is impossible for reality to consist of an infinite succession of dependent beings, it may be helpful here to have a general view of what seems to be the structure of the argument in step two.

1. Something has existed from eternity.

Therefore:

2. Either there is an independent being or there has been an infinite succession of dependent beings.

3. It is impossible that there has been an infinite succession of dependent beings.

Therefore:

4. There is an independent being (i.e., a being that has the reason of its existence within its own nature).

Step one of Clarke's Cosmological Argument gave as a conclusion what here appears as premise (1). We have considered (2) and the inference from (1) to (2). Since (4) clearly follows from (2) and (3), the critical issue in the argument of step two is proposition (3). In the following passage, Clarke presents his argument against an infinite succession of dependent beings.

⟨ For it is plainly impossible, and contradictory to itself. ⟩ I shall not argue against it from the supposed impossibility of infinite succession, barely and absolutely considered in itself; . . . But, if we consider such an infinite progression, as one entire endless series of dependent beings; 'tis plain this whole series of beings can have no cause from without, of its existence; because in it are supposed to be included all things that are or ever were in the universe: And 'tis plain it can have no reason within itself, of its existence; because no one being in this infinite succession is supposed to be self-existent or necessary, (which is the only ground or reason of existence of any thing that can be imagined within the thing itself, as will presently more fully appear,) but every one dependent on the foregoing: . . . An infinite succession therefore of merely dependent beings, without any original independent cause; is a series of beings, that has neither necessity, nor cause, nor any reason or ground at all of its existence, either within itself or from without: That is, 'tis an express contradiction and impossibility; 'tis a supposing something to be caused, (because it is granted in every one of its stages of succession, not to be necessarily and of itself;) and yet that, in the whole, 'tis caused absolutely by nothing (*Demonstration*, pp. 12 13).

In stating "I shall not argue against it from the supposed impossibility of infinite succession, barely and absolutely considered in itself," Clarke sides with Aristotle, Aquinas, and other philosophers in rejecting several arguments for the conclusion that there must have been a *first moment* in the history of the world. Perhaps the best known of these arguments is the one employed by Bonaventure, rejected by Aquinas, defended by Cudworth, and made famous by Kant in the first antinomy.

1. If the world always was, then an infinite number of days has elapsed before the present day.

2. *It is impossible that an infinite number of days has elapsed before the present day.*

Therefore:

3. *It is false that the world always was.*

It is difficult to show exactly what is wrong with this argument. One is inclined to dismiss premise (2). But is it at all clear how the present day could have arrived if an absolutely infinite number of days already had to have come and gone? Indeed, if an infinite number of days has elapsed before the present day, then not only the present day but *any* day in the past could not have occurred unless before it an absolutely infinite number of days had come and gone. G. E. Moore has suggested that the idea expressed in the second premise confronts us with a difficulty analogous to one of the difficulties that makes Zeno's paradox of Achilles and the Tortoise plausible. Thus in discussing Kant's appeal to the argument stated above, Moore remarks, "Just as it seems impossible that Achilles should ever get over an absolutely infinite series of spaces, even though these spaces are constantly diminishing in size; so, I think, it seemed to Kant impossible that time should ever have got over an absolutely infinite series of *hours,* as it must have done in order to get to the present moment."[4] One might contend that the difficulty in the argument put forth by Bonaventure is more severe than in Zeno's paradox. For the infinite series of spaces that Achilles must pass over has a limit. That is, the *sum* of the infinite series of spaces that Achilles must pass over to catch the tortoise is equal to a *finite* length of space. But the infinite series of days—or whatever finite time interval

[4] *Some Main Problems of Philosophy*, p. 181.

we choose—that must have elapsed to arrive at the present day has no limit; that is, the sum of the days having elapsed is not equal to *any* finite length of time.

Since Clarke does not use the argument we have been considering, there is no need here to examine it further. However, one point that has some bearing on our examination of the Cosmological Argument deserves mention. It might be thought that the series of days that has elapsed cannot be infinite since it is the nature of an infinite series not to have an *end*. But if an infinite series of days has elapsed prior to the present day then it would seem that the present day marks the *end* of that series. The mistake here is the assumption that an infinite series cannot have an end. A series may be truly infinite even if it has an end in one direction. The series of numbers 1, 2, 3, 4, 5, etc., is a truly infinite series even though it has an end point in one direction. As Moore remarks:

> There is, therefore, an absolutely infinite series of different numbers starting from the number 1; and this series is truly infinite, in spite of the fact that it has an end in one direction, simply because it has none in the other. It is, therefore, a pure fallacy to suppose that there cannot have been an infinite series of past hours, simply because that series has an end in one direction— has come to an end now: all that we mean by calling it infinite is that it has no end in the other direction or, in other words, no beginning.[5]

Clarke's argument against the possibility of an infinite succession of dependent beings is based on the assumption that there must be a cause or reason for the

[5] *Ibid.*, p. 180.

existence of an infinite succession of dependent beings. This, as we shall see, is an assumption that many philosophers, including Hume, have questioned, if not denied. But for the moment we shall grant the assumption in order to consider another difficulty in Clarke's argument. The reason for the existence of an infinite succession of dependent beings must be found, Clarke infers, either in the causal efficacy of some other being—i.e., a being outside of the succession—or within the nature of the succession itself. If we ask why the reason is not to be found in the causal efficacy of some being outside the infinite succession, Clarke's reply is: "because in it (the infinite succession) are supposed to be included all things that are or ever were in the universe." What this reply shows, I think, is that the argument we are here considering—even if it is a good argument—does not establish that it is impossible that there has been an infinite succession of dependent beings. What the argument, if good, establishes is that *the whole of existing things* cannot consist of an infinite succession of dependent beings. For only if one is trying to prove that it is impossible that the whole of existing things consists of an infinite succession of dependent beings, is it cogent to give the reason Clarke gives for why the succession cannot have its cause in some being outside the succession. In view of this difficulty, perhaps the most reasonable procedure is to restate the general structure of the argument in step two, making the appropriate changes in premises (2) and (3).

1. Something has existed from eternity.

Therefore:

2a. Either there is an independent being or the

Two Criticisms

whole of existing things consists of an infinite succession of dependent beings.

3a. It is impossible that the whole of existing things consists of an infinite succession of dependent beings.

Therefore:

4. There is an independent being (i.e., a being that has the reason of its existence within its own nature).

Of course, having altered the second premise in order to make its second disjunct equivalent to the proposition Clarke's argument purports to show to be impossible, we must reconsider the question whether the second premise—now expressed by (2a)—is derivable from (1), or at least from (1) and PSR. From PSR and (1), it follows that, if there is no independent being, then not only is every being dependent but there has been an infinite succession of dependent beings.[6] However, if this is all that follows from (1) and PSR then what follows is not (2a) but

[6] There is, perhaps, a difficulty here. Since Clarke apparently allows the possibility that *a* may exist by virtue of the causal efficacy of *b* even though *b* does not exist temporally prior to *a*, it would seem consistent with his premise that there be only a *finite succession* of dependent beings in the *temporal order*. That is, *a* may have ceased to exist a thousand years ago, but before that have always existed. Up to the present, on this supposition, there need be only a finite succession of dependent beings in the temporal order. But if we allow the term "succession" to cover not only a series of beings in the temporal order but also a series of beings causally related but existing *simultaneously*, it would still follow that there would have to be an infinite succession of dependent beings. For *a* would have to have its cause in *b* (which did not exist temporally prior to *a*), *b* in *c*, etc.

2b. Either there is an independent being or every being is dependent and there has been an infinite succession of dependent beings.

Although (2a) entails (2b), (2b) does not entail (2a). For it is consistent with (2b) that there be more than one infinite succession of dependent beings. For example, suppose that one man has generated another from eternity and that some other animal, a horse perhaps, has been generated one from another from eternity. Here it seems we would have two infinite successions of dependent beings, the one consisting of the causal series whose members are men, the other consisting of the causal series whose members are horses. But it would then be false that the whole of existing things is contained in any given infinite succession of dependent beings. To avoid this difficulty, we may say (and perhaps Clarke would say) that in this case there is but *one* infinite succession, a succession that has, as it were, two separate causal series as parts. Or, instead, we may speak of an *infinite collection* of dependent beings. If something has existed from eternity and if there is no independent being then, given PSR, it follows that the whole of existing things consists of an infinite collection of dependent beings. The collection would have to contain an infinite number of members, otherwise some member would not be dependent, that is, would not have the reason for its existence in the causal efficacy of some other being.[7] The collection would contain, presumably, any number of causal series, and would be

[7] This will be so only if it is impossible that some being *a* has as its cause a being *b* whose existence is caused by *a* or some being for which *a* is the immediate or remote cause. In short, this will be so only if, in Scotus's phrase, "a circle of causes is inadmissable."

such that there never was a time preceding which no member of the collection was in existence—otherwise it would not be true that something has existed from eternity. Perhaps, then, the best way of accommodating the difficulty that there might be a number of causal series stretching back into the past is to claim that whether or not this be so, it would still be true that from (1) "Something has existed from eternity," and from PSR it follows that

> 2c. *Either there is an independent being or the whole of existing things consists of an infinite collection of dependent beings.*

I suggest that what Clarke's argument is designed to show is that the second disjunct of (2c) expresses an impossibility.

Why is it impossible that the whole of existing things should consist of an infinite collection of dependent beings? The proponent of the Cosmological Argument answers as follows: The infinite collection *itself* requires an explanation of its existence. For since it is true of each member of the collection that it might not have existed, it is true of the whole infinite collection that it might not have existed. But if the entire infinite collection might not have existed, there must be some explanation of why it exists rather than not. The explanation cannot lie in the causal efficacy of some being outside of the collection since by supposition the collection includes every being that is or ever was. Nor can the explanation of why there is an infinite collection be found within the collection itself, for since no member of the collection is independent, has the reason for its existence within itself, the collection as a whole cannot have the reason of its existence within itself. Thus the conception of an infinite collection of dependent beings is the conception of something whose existence has no explanation whatever. But since PSR tells us that whatever exists has an explanation of its existence, either within itself or in the causal efficacy of some other being, it cannot be that the whole of existing things consists of an infinite collection of dependent beings.

The reasoning developed in the last paragraph may be exhibited as follows:

1. If the whole of existing things consists of an infinite collection of dependent beings, then the existence of the infinite collection must have an explanation.

2. If the existence of the infinite collection of dependent beings has an explanation, then the explanation must lie either in the causal efficacy of some being outside the collection or it must lie within the collection itself.

3. The explanation of the existence of the infinite collection of dependent beings cannot lie in the causal efficacy of some being outside the collection.

4. The explanation of the existence of the infinite collection of dependent beings cannot lie within the collection itself.

Therefore:

5. There is no explanation of the infinite collection of dependent beings.

Therefore:

6. It is false that the whole of existing things consists of an infinite collection of dependent beings.

Perhaps every step in this argument is open to criticism. I propose here, however, to consider only two criticisms, criticisms that have achieved some degree of acceptance in the philosophical community. The first of these criticisms is directed at premise (1). According to this criticism, it *makes no sense* to apply the notion of cause or explanation to the totality of things, and the arguments used to show that the whole of existing things must have a cause or explanation are *fallacious.* Thus, in his B.B.C. debate with Father Copleston, Bertrand Russell took the view that the concept of cause is inapplicable to the universe conceived of as the total collection of things. When pressed by Copleston as to how he could rule out "the legitimacy of asking the question how the total, or anything at all comes to be there," Russell responded: "I can illustrate what seems to me your fallacy. Every man who exists has a mother, and it seems to me your argument is that therefore the human race must have a mother, but obviously the human race hasn't a mother—that's a different logical sphere."[8]

The second major criticism is directed at premise (4). According to this criticism, it is intelligible to ask for an explanation of the existence of the infinite collection of dependent beings. But the answer to this question, so the criticism goes, is provided once we learn that each member of the infinite collection has an explanation of its existence. Thus Hume remarks: "Did I show you the particular causes of each individual in a collection of twenty particles of matter, I should think it very unreasonable, should you afterwards ask me, what was the cause of the whole twenty. This is sufficiently explained in explaining the cause of the parts."[9]

[8] "A Debate," p. 175.   [9] *Dialogues*, Part IX.

These two criticisms express, I believe, the major reasons philosophers have given for rejecting the portion of the Cosmological Argument that seeks to establish that the whole of existing things cannot consist of an infinite collection of dependent beings. Let us examine each of these criticisms.

The first criticism draws attention to what appears to be a fatal flaw in the Cosmological Argument. It seems that the proponent of the argument (i) ascribes to the infinite collection itself a property (having a cause or explanation) that is applicable only to the members of that collection, and (ii) does so by means of a fallacious inference from a proposition about the members of the collection to a proposition about the collection itself. There are, then, *two* alleged mistakes committed here. The first error is, perhaps, a category mistake—the ascription to the collection of a property applicable only to the members of the collection. As Russell would say, the collection, in comparison with its members, belongs to a "different logical sphere." The second error apparently explains why the proponent of the Cosmological Argument is led to make the first mistake. He ascribes the property of having an explanation to the infinite collection because he *infers* that the infinite collection must have a cause or explanation from the premise that each of its members has a cause. But this inference, Russell suggests, is as fallacious as to infer that the human race must have a mother because each member of the human race has a mother.

That the proponent of the Cosmological Argument ascribes the property of having a cause or explanation to the infinite collection of dependent beings is certainly true. That to do so is a category mistake is questionable. But before pursuing this point, I want to deal with the second charge. The main question we must consider in connection with the second charge is whether the Cosmological Argument involves the inference: Every member of the infinite collection has an explanation of its existence; therefore, the infinite collection itself has an explanation of its existence. As we have seen, Russell thinks Copleston has employed this inference in concluding that there must be an explanation for the totality of things, and not simply for each of the things making up that totality.

Perhaps some proponents of the Cosmological Argument have used the argument that Russell regards as fallacious. But not all of them have. Moreover, there is no need to employ such an inference, since in PSR the proponent of the Cosmological Argument has available a principle from which it appears to follow that the infinite collection of dependent beings must have an explanation of its existence. Thus Clarke reasons that the infinite collection of beings must have an explanation of its existence by appealing to the strong form of PSR. The principle assures us that whatever exists has an explanation. But if there exists an infinite succession or collection of dependent beings, then that collection or succession, Clarke reasons, must have an explanation of its existence.[10] Hence, we can, I think, safely dismiss the charge that the Cosmological Argument involves an erroneous inference from the premise that every member of the infinite collection has an explanation to the conclusion that the collection itself must have an explanation of its existence.

We must now deal with the question whether it makes *sense* to ascribe the property of having an ex-

[10] See pp. 144-151 for a further consideration of the application of PSR to the infinite collection of dependent beings.

planation or cause to the infinite collection of dependent beings. Clearly only if it does make sense is Clarke's reasoning in connection with step two of his argument acceptable. Our question, then, is whether it makes sense to ask for a cause or explanation of the entire universe, conceiving of the universe as an infinite collection of dependent beings.

Ronald Hepburn, one recent critic of the Cosmological Argument, has stated our problem as follows:

> When we are seriously speaking of absolutely everything there is, are we speaking of something that requires a cause, in the way that events *in* the universe may require causes? What indeed can be safely said at all about the totality of things? For a great many remarks that one can make with perfect propriety about limited things quite obviously can *not* be made about the cosmos itself. It cannot, for instance, be said meaningfully to be 'above' or 'below' anything, although things-in-the-universe can be so related to one another. Whatever we might claim to be *'below* the universe' would turn out to be just some more *universe.* We should have been relating part to part, instead of relating the whole to something not-the-universe. The same applies to 'outside the universe.' We can readily imagine a boundary, a garden wall, shall we say, round something that we want to call the universe. But if we imagine ourselves boring a hole through that wall and pushing a stick out *beyond* it into a nameless zone 'outside,' we should still not in fact have given meaning to the phrase 'outside the universe.' For the place into which the stick was intruding would deserve to be called a part of the universe (even if consisting of empty space, no matter) just as much as the area within

the walls. We should have demonstrated *not* that the universe has an outside, but that what we took to be the whole universe was not really the whole. Our problem is this. Supposing we could draw up a list of questions that can be asked about objects in the universe, but cannot be asked about the *whole* universe: Would the question, 'Has it a cause?' be on that list? One thing is clear. Whether or not this question is on the proscribed list, we are not entitled to argue as the Cosmological Argument does that *because* things in the world have causes, therefore the sum of things must also have *its* cause. No more (as we have just seen) can we argue from the fact that things in the world have tops and bottoms, insides and outsides, and are related to other things, to the belief that the universe has *its* top and bottom, inside and outside, and is related to a supra-cosmical something.[11]

In this passage Hepburn (i) points out that some properties (e.g., "above," "below") of things in the universe cannot properly be ascribed to the total universe, (ii) raises the question whether "having a cause" is such a property, and (iii) concludes that ". . . we are not entitled to argue as the Cosmological Argument does that *because* things in the world have causes, therefore, the sum of things must also have *its* cause." We noted earlier that the Cosmological Argument (i.e., the version we are examining) does not argue that the sum of things (the infinite collection of dependent beings) must have a cause *because* each thing has a cause. Thus we may safely ignore Hepburn's main objection. However, his other two points are well taken. There certainly are

[11] Ronald W. Hepburn, *Christianity and Paradox* (London: Watts, 1958), pp. 167-168.

properties that it makes sense to apply to things within a collection but make no sense when applied to the collection itself. What assurance do we have that "having a cause" is not such a property?

Suppose we are holding in our hands a collection of ten marbles. Not only would each marble have a definite weight but the collection itself would have a weight. Indeed, from the premise that each marble weighs more than one ounce we could infer validly that the collection itself weighs more than an ounce. This example shows that it is not always fallacious to infer that a collection has a certain property from the premise that each member of the collection has that property.[12] But the collection in this example is, we might say, *concrete* rather than *abstract*. That is, we are here considering the collection as itself a physical entity, an aggregate of marbles. This, of course, is not a collection in the sense of a *class* or *set* of things. Holding several marbles in my hands I can consider the set whose members are those marbles. The set itself, being an *abstract* entity, rather than a physical heap, has no weight. Just as the set of human beings has no mother, so the set whose members are marbles in my hand has no weight. Therefore, in considering whether it makes sense to speak of the infinite collection of dependent beings as having a cause or explanation of its existence it is important to decide whether we are speaking of a collection as a *concrete* entity—for example, a physical whole or aggregate—or as an *abstract* entity.

Suppose we view the infinite collection of dependent beings as itself a concrete entity. So far as the Cosmologi-

[12] For a consideration of inferences of this sort in connection with the fallacy of composition see my paper, "The Fallacy of Composition," *Mind*, Vol. LXXI, No. 281 (January 1964).

cal Argument is concerned, one advantage of so viewing it is that it is understandable why it might have
the property of having a cause or explanation of its
existence. For concrete entities—physical objects,
events, physical heaps—can be caused. Thus if the infinite collection is a concrete entity it may well make
sense to ascribe to it the property of having a cause or
explanation.

But such a view of the infinite collection is implausible, if not plainly incorrect. Many collections of physical things cannot possibly be themselves *concrete* entities. Think, for example, of the collection whose
members are the largest prehistoric beast, Socrates, and
the Empire State Building. By any stretch of the imagination can we view this collection as itself a concrete
thing? Clearly we cannot. Such a collection must be
construed as an *abstract* entity, a class or set.[13] But if
there are many collections of beings that cannot be concrete entities, what grounds have we for thinking that,
on the supposition that every being that is or ever was
is dependent, the collection of those beings would itself
be a concrete thing such as a physical heap. At best our
knowledge of the things (both past and present) com-
prising the universe and our knowledge of their inter-
relations would have to be much greater before we
would be entitled to view the *sum* of concrete things,
past and present, as itself something *concrete*.

But if the infinite collection of dependent beings is to

[13] Of course, the three members of this collection, unlike the
members of the collection of dependent beings, presumably are
causally unrelated. But it is equally easy to think of collections
that cannot possibly be concrete entities whose members are
causally related—e.g., the collection whose members are the ances-
tors of a given man.

be understood as an *abstract* entity, say the set whose members include all the beings that are or ever were, have not we conceded the point to Russell? A set or class conceived of as an abstract entity has no weight, is not below or above anything, and cannot be thought of as being caused or brought into being. Thus if the infinite collection is a set, an abstract entity, is not Russell right in charging that it makes no more sense to ascribe the property of having a cause or an explanation to the infinite collection itself than it does to ascribe the property of having a mother to the human race?

Suppose that every being that is or ever was is dependent. Suppose further that the number of such beings is infinite. Let A be the set consisting of these beings. Thus no being exists or ever existed that is not a member of A. Does it make sense to ask for an explanation of A's existence? We do, of course, ask questions about sets that are equivalent to questions about their members. For example, "Is set X included in set Y?" is equivalent to the question "Is every member of X a member of Y?" I suggest that the question "Why does A exist?" be taken to mean "Why does A have the members that it does rather than some other members or none at all?" Consider, for example, the set of men. Let M be this set. The question "Why does M exist?" is perhaps odd if we understand it as a request for an explanation of the existence of an abstract entity. But the question "Why does M exist?" may be taken to mean "Why does M have the members it does rather than some other members or none at all?" So understood, the form of words "Why does M exist?" does ask an intelligible question. It is a contingent fact that Hitler existed. Indeed, it is a contingent fact that any men exist at all. One of Leibniz's logically possible worlds is a world that includes some members of M— for example, Socrates and Plato—but not others—say Hitler and Stalin. Another is a world in which the set of men is entirely empty and therefore identical with the null set.[14] Why is it, then, that M exists? That is, why does M have just the members it does rather than some other members or none at all? Not only is this question intelligible but we seem to have some idea of what its answer is. Presumably, the theory of evolution might be a part of the explanation of why M is not included in the null set and why its members have certain properties rather than others.

But if the question "Why does M exist?" makes sense, why should not the question "Why does A exist?" also make sense? A is the set of dependent beings. In asking why A exists, we are not asking for an explanation of the existence of an abstract entity, we are asking why A has the members it has rather than some other members or none at all? I submit that this question does make sense. Moreover, I think it is precisely this question that the proponents of the Cosmological Argument were posing when they asked for an explanation of the existence of the infinite collection or succession of dependent

[14] These remarks, I think, are true of possible worlds, but not true of Leibniz's view of possible worlds. If I understand Leibniz correctly, his view implies that there is no identity through possible worlds. Each possible world containing objects has *different* objects from every other possible world. If so, then no other possible world contains Socrates and Plato. The view I am suggesting does allow for identity of objects through possible worlds. This view is not without difficulties. See, for example, Roderick M. Chisholm, "Identity Through Possible Worlds: Some Questions," *Nous*, Vol. I (1967), pp. 1-8.

beings.[15] Of course, it is one thing for a question to make sense and another thing for there to be an answer to it.

The interpretation I have given to the question "Why does A exist?" is somewhat complex. For according to this interpretation, what is being asked is not simply why does A have members rather than having none, but also why does A have just the members it does rather than having some other members. Although the proponents of the Cosmological Argument do seem to interpret the question in this way, it will facilitate our discussion if we simplify the interpretation somewhat by focusing our attention solely on the question why A has the members it has rather than having none. Hence, for purposes of simplification, in what follows I shall take the question "Why does A exist?" to mean "Why does A have the members it has rather than not having any?"

For any being to be a member of A it is necessary and sufficient that it have the reason for its existence in the causal efficacy of some other being. Imagine the following state of affairs. A has exactly three members: a_1, a_2, and a_3. The last member, a_3, exists by reason of the causal efficacy of a_2, and a_2 exists by reason of the causal efficacy of a_1. There exists an *eternal* being b that does not exist by reason of the causal efficacy of any other being. Since b is not a dependent being, b is not a member of A. At a certain time a_1 came into existence by

[15] For example, in speaking of the infinite succession, Hume has Demea say: "and yet it is evident that it requires a cause or reason, as much as any particular object which begins to exist in time. The question is still reasonable, why this particular succession of causes existed from eternity, and not any other succession, or no succession at all" (*Dialogues*, Part IX).

reason of the causal efficacy of *b*. Clearly the question "Why does A exist?" when taken to mean "Why does A have the members it has rather than none at all?" makes sense when asked within the context of this imagined state of affairs. Indeed, part of the answer to the question would involve reference to *b* and its causal efficacy in bringing about the existence of one of the members of A, namely a_1.

What this case shows is that the question "Why does A exist?" is not always (i.e., in every context) meaningless. If Russell holds that the question is meaningless in the framework of the Cosmological Argument, it must be because of some special assumption about A that forms part of the context of the Cosmological Argument. The assumption in question undoubtedly is that absolutely every being is dependent. On this assumption, every being that is or ever was has membership in A, and A has an infinite number of members.

Perhaps Russell's view is that within the context of the assumption that *every* being is dependent it makes no sense to ask why A has the members it has rather than none at all. It makes no sense, he might argue, for two reasons. First, on the assumption that every being is dependent, there could not be such a thing as the *set* A whose members are all dependent beings. For the set A is, although abstract, presumably a being. But if every being is dependent, then A would have to be dependent and therefore a member of itself. But apart from whatever difficulties arise when a set is said to be a member of itself, it would seem to make little sense to think of an abstract entity, such as a set, as being caused, as having the reason of its existence within the causal efficacy of some other being.

Second, Russell might argue that the assumption that

every being is dependent and therefore a member of A rules out the *possibility* of any answer to the question why A has the members it has rather than none at all. For on that assumption our question about A is in effect a question about the totality of things. And, as Russell observes, "I see no reason whatsoever to suppose that the total has any cause whatsoever."[16]

Neither of these reasons suffices to show that our question about A is meaningless. The first reason does, however, point up the necessity of introducing some restriction on the assumption "Every being is dependent" in order that abstract entities like numbers and sets not fall within the scope of the expression "Every being" as that expression occurs in the assumption "Every being is dependent." Such a restriction will obviate the difficulty that A is said to be both a member of itself and dependent. I propose the following rough restriction. In speaking of beings, we shall restrict ourselves to beings that *could be caused* to exist by some other being or *could be causes* of the existence of other beings. God (if He exists), a man, the sun, a stone are beings of this sort. Presumably, numbers sets and the like are not. The assumption that every being is dependent is to be understood under this restriction. That is, we are here assuming that every being *of the sort described by the restriction* is in fact a being that exists by reason of the causal efficacy of some other being.

The second reason given confuses the issue of whether a question makes sense, is meaningful, with the issue of whether a question has an answer. Of course, given the assumption that every being (of the sort described by the restriction) is a member of A, we cannot expect to find the cause or reason of A's existence in some be-

[16] "A Debate," p. 176.

ing that is not a member of A. If the explanation of A's existence cannot be found within A itself, then we must conclude that there can be no explanation of the infinite collection of dependent beings. But this is to say only that, on our assumption that every being is dependent, there is no answer to the question "Why does A exist?" It is one thing for a question not to have an answer and quite another thing for the question to be meaningless.

It can be shown that it is incorrect to conclude that a question is meaningless from the premise that there is no answer to it. Putting aside PSR, let us suppose that the world came into existence at a certain moment *t* prior to which nothing existed. That is, let us suppose that the question "What caused the world to come into existence at *t*?" has no answer at all. On this supposition it will, of course, be false that God exists and caused the world to come into existence at *t*. But, although false, the proposition "God exists and caused the world to come into existence at *t*" is not *self-contradictory*. Consider, then, the following propositions:

1. *God exists and caused the world to come into existence at t.*
2. *It is logically possible that God exists and caused the world to come into existence at t.*
3. *The world came into existence at t.*
4. *Nothing caused the world to come into existence at t.*

The conjunction of (1), (3), and (4) constitutes an inconsistent triad. But the conjunction of (2), (3), and (4) is not inconsistent. They may all be true. But since this is so, it follows that the question "What caused the world to come into existence at *t*?" *makes sense*. For consider the following argument:

141

1. *If God exists and caused the world to come into existence at* t *then the question "What caused the world to come into existence at* t*?" has an answer.*
2. *It is logically possible that God exists and caused the world to come into existence at* t.

Therefore:

3. *It is logically possible that the question "What caused the world to come into existence at* t*?" has an answer.*
4. *If it is logically possible that a question has an answer then that question is meaningful.*

Therefore:

5. *The question "What caused the world to come into existence at* t*?" is meaningful.*

This argument is unaffected by the assumption that nothing caused the world to come into existence at *t*. For as we saw above, that assumption is *consistent* with proposition (2). Thus there is no *inconsistency* in holding that the question "What caused the world to come into existence at *t*?" is meaningful and yet has no answer.

Premise (4) is, perhaps, questionable. But its contrapositive certainly seems true, and I cannot think of any reasons for thinking it false. (4) is logically equivalent to the proposition "If a question is not meaningful then it is logically impossible that it has an answer." Surely if a question lacks meaning then it asks nothing. And if a certain question asks nothing then not only is there in fact no answer to what it asks but it is impossible that there should be. Only if a question asks something is it possible for there to be an answer to what it asks.

I have been arguing that although our assumption that every being is a member of A implies that there is no answer to the question "Why does A exist?" it does not imply that the question is meaningless. In addition I have argued that, *if* it is logically possible that God exists and made it to be that A has the members it does, then it is logically possible that the question "Why does A exist?" has an answer. Is it, then, logically possible that God exists and made it to be that A has the members it in fact has?

Some philosophers have argued that it is impossible for there to exist a being with the properties (absolute goodness, power, knowledge, etc.) essential to God. But it would take us far beyond the scope of this study to examine their arguments. I shall here *assume* that it is logically possible both that God exists and that God made it to be that A has the members it in fact has. If we make this assumption then we must admit that the question "Why does A exist?"—i.e., "Why does A have the members it does rather than none at all?"—is *meaningful*.

We have been examining the first of the two major criticisms philosophers have directed at the reasoning by which the Cosmological Argument endeavors to establish that it is impossible that the whole of existing things consists of an infinite collection of dependent beings. The heart of this criticism is that it *makes no sense* to ascribe the property of having a cause or explanation to the infinite collection of dependent beings. This criticism, I think, has been shown to be correct in one way, but incorrect in another. If we construe the infinite collection of dependent beings as an abstract entity, a set, it perhaps does not make sense to claim that something caused the existence of this abstract entity. But the question "Why does A exist?" may be understood to mean "Why does A have the members it does rather than none at all?" I have argued that, taken in this way, the question "Why does A exist?" is a *meaningful* question.

According to PSR there must be an answer to the question "Why does A exist?"—an explanation of the existence of the infinite collection of dependent beings. Moreover, the explanation must lie either in the causal efficacy of some being outside of the collection or within the collection itself. But since by supposition every being is dependent—and therefore in the collection—there is no being outside the collection whose causal efficacy might explain the existence of the collection. Therefore, either the collection has the explanation of its existence within itself *or* there can be no explanation of its existence. If the first alternative is rejected then, since PSR requires that everything has an explanation of its existence, we must reject the supposition that every being is dependent. For on that assumption there is no explanation of why there is an infinite collection of dependent beings.

Before turning to an examination of the second major criticism, we need to reconsider the connection between PSR and A, the set of dependent beings. Earlier I suggested that Russell, Hepburn, and others are mistaken in assuming that the Cosmological Argument contains the inference: Every member of the collection of dependent beings has an explanation of its existence; therefore, the collection itself has an explanation of its existence. Instead, I suggested that Clarke reasons that the infinite collection of dependent beings must have an explanation by appealing to the strong form of PSR. For that principle assures us that whatever exists must have an explanation of its existence. And if there exists an infinite succession or collection of dependent beings, then that collection, Clarke thinks, must have an explanation of its existence. But in view of the interpretation I have given to the assertion that A (the set of dependent beings) exists, we must reconsider the question of whether the strong form of PSR entitles us to conclude that there must be an explanation for the existence of the infinite collection of dependent beings.

In trying to interpret Clarke's view of the infinite collection of dependent beings, I first suggested that if the collection itself is construed as a physical heap or aggregate then the application of PSR to it is reasonable. This suggestion, however, was discarded because it seems we have no good reasons to think that, on the supposition that every being that is or ever was is dependent, the collection of those beings would be a *concrete* entity such as a physical heap. Instead, I suggested that we view the collection of dependent beings as itself an abstract entity, a class or set. I then argued that we may view the sentence "Why does the set of dependent beings exist?" as ambiguous. For on the one hand it could be construed as asking why there is a certain abstract entity, the set of dependent beings. But on the other hand it could be construed as asking why this abstract entity, the set of dependent beings, has the members it does rather than none at all. I argued that it is the second interpretation of the question "Why does the set of dependent beings exist?" that best reflects the views of the proponents of the Cosmological Argument. The question I am now raising is whether, given this interpretation, it follows from the strong form of PSR that there must be an explanation of the existence of the set of dependent beings.

The strong form of PSR says that every existing thing has an explanation of its existence. It is natural to infer from this that if there exists an infinite collection of dependent beings then there must be an explanation of the fact that *it* exists. But we must remember that, on the interpretation we are pursuing, the assertion that there exists a set (collection) of dependent beings does *not* assert the existence of a certain being or thing. What it asserts (roughly) is that the set of dependent beings has members. The question, then, is whether from

> a. *Every existing being has an explanation of its existence either in the causal efficacy of some other being or within the necessity of its own nature.*

it follows that

> b. *If the set of dependent beings has members there is an explanation of the fact that it has members rather than not.*

It must be admitted that the question I am now raising is one that did not occur to the eighteenth-century proponents of the Cosmological Argument. The reason for this, I think, is that the proponents of the argument never saw clearly that the infinite collection of dependent beings is not itself a dependent being. They tended to confuse the question of why the set of dependent beings has members (rather than not having any) with the altogether different question of why a certain being exists. Thus in considering the view that the infinite succession of dependent beings might *itself* not have an explanation, Clarke remarks: " 'Tis in reality, and in point of argument the very same supposition; as it would be to suppose one continued being, of beginningless and endless duration, neither self-existent and necessary in itself, nor having its existence founded in any self-existent cause. Which is directly absurd and contradictory" (*Demonstration*, pp. 13-14).

This same confusion persists in the writings of contemporary defenders of the Cosmological Argument. Richard Taylor, for example, speaks of "the world" as the totality of existing things (excluding God, if He exists), and even points out that we cannot infer that this totality has an explanation from the fact that each of its members does: "It is not logically necessary that a totality should share the defects of its members. For example, even though every man is mortal, it does not follow from this that the human race, or the totality of all men, is also mortal; for it is possible that there will always be human beings, even though there are no human beings that will always exist."[17] But having treated the world as the collection of existing things (excepting God), Taylor, like Clarke, proceeds to view it as an existing thing subject to the very same PSR that applies to its members. "But it is at least very odd and arbitrary to deny of this existing world the need for any sufficient reason, whether independent of itself or not, while presupposing that there is a reason for every *other thing* that ever exists."[18]

Clearly, if to ask of the infinite collection of dependent beings why it exists is no different from asking of some particular being why it exists, then the form of PSR that suffices to require an explanation of the latter will suffice to require an explanation of the former. But,

[17] *Metaphysics*, pp. 91-92.   [18] *Ibid.*, p. 87. Italics mine.

as we have seen, to ask why the infinite collection of dependent beings exists is, in part, to ask why it has members rather than not having any. And the version of PSR Clarke presents (i.e., Every being must have an explanation of its existence) does not imply that there must be an explanation of the fact that a certain set has members. If every existing being must have an explanation of its existence, then there must be an explanation of the existence of each member of the set of dependent beings. But must there be an explanation of the fact that the set of dependent beings has members? Perhaps there must. But *that* there must does not follow from PSR as Clarke formulates it for the Cosmological Argument.

Richard Taylor provides two distinct versions of PSR. He first presents PSR as the belief "that there is some explanation for the existence of anything whatever, some reason why it should exist rather than not."[19] This statement of PSR is, I think, equivalent to what I have earlier called the strong form of PSR. For our purposes, it need not be distinguished from Clarke's statement of PSR. But this version of PSR, as I have indicated above, is insufficient for the Cosmological Argument. It is insufficient because it does not imply that there must be an explanation of the fact that the set of dependent beings has members rather than not. And unless there must be an explanation for this fact, we cannot prove that it is impossible for the whole of existing things to consist of an infinite collection of dependent beings.

Taylor's second statement of PSR is much more general and does, I believe, imply that there must be an

19 *Ibid.*, p. 85.

explanation of the fact that the set of dependent beings has members. He remarks:

> The principle involved here has been called the principle of sufficient reason. Actually, it is a very general principle, and is best expressed by saying that, in the case of any positive truth, there is some sufficient reason for it, something which, in this sense, makes it true— in short, that there is some sort of explanation, known or unknown, for everything.[20]

This version of PSR, however, is too strong. For it implies that there must be an explanation for every actual state of affairs. And, as we saw earlier, any version of PSR that has this implication is implausible, if not demonstratively false.

Taylor's two versions of PSR are substantially no different from the two versions we considered earlier:

PSR_1: *Every actual state of affairs has a reason either within itself or in some other state of affairs.*

PSR_2: *Every existing thing has a reason for its existence either in the necessity of its own nature or in the causal efficacy of some other being.*

What we have seen is that, on our interpretation of what it is to explain the existence of the infinite collection of dependent beings, PSR_2 does not imply that there must be an explanation of the existence of the collection of dependent beings. PSR_1 does have this implication. For if the state of affairs constituted by the set of dependent beings having members is an actual state of

---

[20] *Ibid.*, p. 86.

affairs then, from PSR_1, it follows that there is an explanation of that state of affairs. We cannot, however, save the Cosmological Argument by appealing to PSR_1—for, as we saw earlier, PSR_1 appears to be false.

Perhaps the best move for the proponent of the Cosmological Argument to make at this juncture is to formulate a version of PSR that will yield the desired result concerning the collection of dependent beings but which will not fall victim to the argument against PSR_1. It will not do to say simply that in addition to PSR_2 we will appeal to PSR_3.

> PSR_3: For every set that has members there must be an explanation of the fact that it has members.

PSR_3, like PSR_1, is too strong. For consider the set of actual, contingent, positive states of affairs. To explain why that set has members rather than not is tantamount to explaining why there are contingent, positive states of affairs. And, as we saw earlier, it seems that there cannot be any explanation of the fact that there are contingent, positive states of affairs.

The above considerations naturally suggest PSR_4.

> PSR_4: For every set whose members are existing beings (which can be caused to exist or which can cause the existence of other beings) there must be an explanation of the fact that it has members.

PSR_4 does not imply that every positive state of affairs has an explanation. Hence, it is not subject to the objection that refutes PSR_3. PSR_4, however, does imply that there must be an explanation of the existence of the infinite collection of dependent beings. And this, along with PSR$_2$, appears to be all the proponent of the Cosmological Argument needs to establish the crucial premise in the Cosmological Argument, namely, that it is not the case that the whole of existing things consists of an infinite collection of dependent beings.

We have been considering the first of two criticisms directed against the reasoning in support of the proposition that it is false that the whole of existing things consists of an infinite collection of dependent beings. The second criticism argues that the proponent of the Cosmological Argument is mistaken in thinking that the explanation of the existence of the infinite collection cannot be found within the collection itself. The explanation of the existence of the collection is provided, so the criticism goes, once we learn what the explanation is of each of the members of the collection. As we noted earlier, this criticism was succinctly expressed by Hume in his remark: "Did I show you the particular causes of each individual in a collection of twenty particles of matter, I should think it very unreasonable, should you afterwards ask me, what was the cause of the whole twenty. This is sufficiently explained in explaining the cause of the parts." Applying this objection to the infinite collection of dependent beings, we obtain the result that to explain the existence of the infinite collection, A, amounts to no more than explaining the existence of each of its members. Now, of course, A is unlike Hume's collection of twenty particles in that we cannot give an infinite number of explanations. But our inability to give a particular explanation for each of the members of A does not imply that there is any member of A for whose existence there is no explanation. Indeed, from the fact that each member of A is dependent (i.e., has the reason for its existence in the causal efficacy of some other being) we know that every member of A has an explanation of its existence, and from the assumption that every being is a member of A we know that for each member of A the explanation lies in the causal efficacy of some other member of A. But, so the criticism goes, if every member of A has an explanation of its existence then the existence of A has been sufficiently explained. For to explain why a certain collection of things exists it is sufficient to explain the existence of each of its members. Hence, since we know that the existence of every one of A's members is explained, we know that the existence of the collection A is explained.

This forceful criticism, originally advanced by Hume, has gained wide acceptance in contemporary philosophy. Indeed, the only remaining problem seems to be to explain why the proponents of the Cosmological Argument failed to see that to explain the existence of all the members of a collection is to explain the existence of the collection. In restating Hume's criticism, Paul Edwards suggests that perhaps they may have been misled by grammar.

> The demand to find the cause of the series as a whole rests on the erroneous assumption that the series is something over and above the members of which it is composed. It is tempting to suppose this, at least by implication, because the word 'series' is a noun like 'dog' or 'man.' Like the expression 'this dog' or 'this man' the phrase 'this series' is easily taken to designate an individual object. But reflection shows this to be an error. If we have explained the individual members there is nothing additional left to be explained. Suppose I see a group of five Eskimos standing on the

corner of Sixth Avenue and 50th Street and I wish to explain why the group came to New York. Investigation reveals the following stories:

Eskimo No. 1 did not enjoy the extreme cold in the polar region and decided to move to a warmer climate.

No. 2 is the husband of Eskimo No. 1. He loves her dearly and did not wish to live without her.

No. 3 is the son of Eskimos 1 and 2. He is too small and too weak to oppose his parents.

No. 4 saw an advertisement in the *New York Times* for an Eskimo to appear on television.

No. 5 is a private detective engaged by the Pinkerton Agency to keep an eye on Eskimo No. 4.

Let us assume that we have now explained in the case of each of the five Eskimos why he or she is in New York. Somebody then asks: "All right, but what about the group as a whole; why is *it* in New York?" This would plainly be an absurd question. There is no group over and above the five members, and if we have explained why each of the five members is in New York we have *ipso facto* explained why the group is there. It is just as absurd to ask for the cause of the series as a whole as distinct from asking for the causes of the individual members.[21]

The principle underlying the Hume-Edwards criticism may be stated as follows: *If the existence of every member of a set is explained the existence of that set is*

[21] Paul Edwards, "The Cosmological Argument," Donald R. Burrill, ed., *The Cosmological Arguments* (New York: Doubleday & Company, Inc., 1967), pp. 113-114. Edwards's paper was originally published in *The Rationalist Annual* for 1959.

thereby explained. This principle seems to be a corollary of our interpretation of the question "Why does this set exist?" For on our interpretation, once it is explained why the set has the members it has rather than none at all, it is thereby explained why the set exists. And it would seem that if a set A has, say, three members, a_1, a_2, and a_3, then if we explain the existence of a_1, a_2, and a_3, we have explained why A has the members it has rather than none at all. Thus the principle that underlies the second major criticism seems to be implied by our conception of what is involved in explaining the existence of a set.

The principle underlying the Hume-Edwards criticism seems plausible enough when restricted to finite sets, i.e., sets with a finite number of members. But the principle is false, I believe, when extended to infinite sets in which the explanation of each member's existence is found in the causal efficacy of some other member. Consider M, the set of men. Suppose M consists of an infinite number of members, each member owing its existence to some other member which generated it. Suppose further that to explain the existence of a given man it is sufficient to note that he was begotten by some other man. That is, where x and y are men and x begat y we allow that the existence of y is explained by the causal efficacy of x. On these suppositions it is clear that the antecedent of the principle is satisfied with respect to M. Every member of M has an explanation of its existence. But does it follow that the existence of M has an explanation? I think not. We do not have an explanation of the existence of M until we have an explanation of why M has the members it has rather than none at all. But clearly if *all* we know is that there always have been men and that every man's existence is explained by the causal efficacy of some other man, we do not know *why* there always have been men rather than none at all. If I ask why M has the members it does rather than none, it is no answer to say that M always had members. We may, I suppose, answer the question "Why does M have the *presently existing* members it has?" by saying that M always had members and there were men who generated the presently existing men. But in asking why M has the members it does rather than none at all, we are not asking why M has the presently existing members it has. To make this clear, we may rephrase our question as follows: "Why is it that M has now and always had members rather than never having had any members at all?" Surely we have not learned the answer to this question when we have learned that there always have been members of M and that each member's existence is explained by the causal efficacy of some other member.

What we have just seen is that, from the fact that the existence of each member of a collection is explained, it does not follow that the existence of the collection is thereby explained. It does not follow because when the collection (set) has an infinite number of members, each member's existence having its explanation in the causal efficacy of *some other member*, it is true that the existence of every member has an explanation and yet still an open question whether the existence of the set has an explanation. To explain the existence of the set we must explain why it has the members it has rather than none. But clearly if every member's existence is explained by some other *member*, then although the existence of every member has an explanation it is still unexplained why the set has the members it has, rather than none at all.

Put somewhat differently, we have seen that the fact (assuming for the moment that it is a fact) that there always have been men, each man's existence brought about by some other man, is insufficient to explain *why* it is a fact that there always have been men rather than a fact that there never have been any men. If someone asks us to explain why there always have been men rather than never having been any, it would not suffice for us to observe that there always have been men and each man has been brought into existence by some other man.

I have argued that the second major criticism rests on a false principle, namely, that, if the existence of every member of a set is explained, then the existence of that set is explained. This principle, so far as I can determine, is true when restricted to sets with a *finite* number of members. For example, if a set A has two members, a_1 and a_2, and if we explain a_2 by a_1 and a_1 by some being b that caused a_1, then we have explained the existence of A. In any case, we have explained why A has members rather than none at all. Thus I am not claiming that the principle underlying Hume's objection is always false. Indeed, as I have just indicated, it is easy to provide an example of a finite set of which the principle is true. And perhaps it is just this feature of the principle—i.e., its plausibility when applied to finite sets such as Hume's collection of twenty particles and Edwards's five Eskimos—that has led Hume and many philosophers since Hume to reject the Cosmological Argument's thesis that, even if every member of the infinite succession of dependent beings has an explanation, the infinite succession itself is not thereby explained. If so, then the mistake Hume and his successors have made is to assume that a principle that is true of all finite sets also is true of all infinite sets.

We know, for example, that, if we have a set B consisting of five members and a set C consisting of three of the members of B, the members of C cannot be put in one-to-one correspondence with those of B. If we reflect on this fact, it is tempting to conclude that for *any* two sets X and Y, if all the members of X are members of Y but some members of Y are not members of X, then the members of X cannot be put in one-to-one correspondence with those of Y. Indeed, so long as X and Y are restricted to *finite* sets, the principle just stated is true. But if we let X be the set of *even* natural numbers—2, 4, 6, . . .—and Y be the set of natural numbers—1, 2, 3, . . .—the principle is shown to be false. For although all the members of X are members of Y and some members of Y—the odd integers—are not members of X, it is not true that the members of X cannot be put in one-to-one correspondence with those of Y. What this example illustrates is that a principle that holds of all finite sets may not hold of all infinite sets. The principle underlying the second major criticism is, I have argued, such a principle.

One point concerning my reply to the second major criticism needs to be made clear. In rejecting the principle on which the criticism rests, I have contended that when a set has an *infinite* number of members, every one of which has an explanation of its existence, it *does not follow* that the existence of the set is thereby explained. In saying this, I do not mean to imply that in explaining the existence of every member of an infinite set we *never* thereby explain the existence of the set, only that we *sometimes* do not. Specifically, we do not,

I think, when we explain the existence of each member of the set by some other member of *that set*. Recall our example of M, the set of men. If we think of the members of this set as forming a temporal series stretching infinitely back in time, each member's existence explained by the causal efficacy of the preceding member, we have an example in which an explanation of the existence of each member of M does not constitute an explanation of the existence of M. But if we let our imagination run free, we can alter our example in such a way that in explaining the existence of each of the infinitely many members of M we do thereby explain the existence of M. Let us suppose that each man is produced not by another man but by some superior being, say a god. What we are supposing is that M is described as before except that, instead of every member having the explanation of its existence in some preceding member of M, the explanation is found in the causal efficacy of some member of the set of gods. From eternity, then, gods have been producing men. There have always been members of M and every member has an explanation of its existence. Here it does seem true to say that in explaining the existence of every member of M we have thereby explained the existence of M. If someone asks why there now are and always have been men rather than never having been any, we respond that there always have been men because there always have been gods producing them. This, if true, would explain why M has always had members.

We have seen that it may be true that the existence of each member in a set is explained, and yet false that the existence of that set is explained. What, then, is sufficient to explain the existence of a set? In interpreting the reasoning of the eighteenth-century proponents of the Cosmological Argument, I suggested that we understand the question of why a certain collection or set exists as follows: Why does the collection (set) have the members it does rather than none at all? This question, admittedly complex, asks why each of the members of the set exists and why the set has any members at all. Accordingly, to explain the existence of a set is (i) to explain the existence of each member of the set, and (ii) to explain why the set has any members at all.

The mistake that underlies the Hume-Edwards criticism is the assumption that, *whenever* one explains the existence of each member of a collection (set), one *thereby* explains why that set has any members at all. As we have seen, whenever a set is such that each member's existence is explained by the causal efficacy of some other member of *that set*, it will be true that we have an explanation of the existence of each member, but false that we thereby have an explanation of why the set has any members at all. And, as I have suggested, it is precisely this point that the proponents of the Cosmological Argument perceive when they say that the reason for the infinite collection of dependent beings cannot be found within the collection but must be sought elsewhere. As Leibniz remarks:

> And even if you imagine the world eternal, nevertheless since you posit nothing but a succession of states, and as you find a sufficient reason for them in none of them whatsoever, and as any number of them whatever does not aid you in giving a reason for them, it is evident that the reason must be sought elsewhere.[22]

---

[22] "On the Ultimate Origin of Things" in Philip P. Wiener, ed., *Leibniz Selections* (New York: Charles Scribner's Sons, 1951), p. 346.

And Clarke, in considering the supposition that the whole of existing things consists of an infinite collection of dependent beings, remarks:

> According to this latter supposition; there is nothing, in the universe, self-existent or necessarily-existing. And if so, then it was originally equally possible, that from eternity there should never have existed any thing at all; as that there should from eternity have existed a succession of changeable and dependent beings. Which being supposed; then, what is it that has from eternity determined such a succession of beings to exist, rather than that from eternity there should never have existed anything at all? *Necessity* it was not; because it was equally possible, in this supposition, that they should not have existed at all. *Chance*, is nothing but a mere word, without any signification. And *other being* 'tis supposed there was none, to determine the existence of these (*Demonstration*, p. 14).

Although I think the proponents of the Cosmological Argument are right in their contention that the supposition that every being is dependent leaves us with no explanation of the existence of the infinite collection (set) of dependent beings, there is, I think, a *logical leap* in their reasoning to this conclusion. This leap is explicit in Clarke's remark and implicit in Leibniz's account of the Cosmological Argument. Indeed, the logical leap is explicit in my own attempt to explicate the reasoning by which Clarke supports his view that it is impossible for the whole of existing things to consist of an infinite collection of dependent beings. For earlier I said: ". . . since it is true of each member of the collection that it might not have existed, it is true of the

whole infinite collection that it might not have existed."
Let us examine this inference and see why it contains a
logical leap.

The inference I made in explicating Clarke's reasoning may be expressed as follows:

> *P. If for every member of the collection of depend-
> ent beings it is possible that it doesn't exist then
> it is possible that every member of the collection
> of dependent beings doesn't exist.*

That Clarke makes this inference is, I think, clear. For
he claims that if no being is necessary—i.e., if for every
being it is possible that it does not exist—then "it was
originally equally possible that from eternity there
should never have existed any thing at all; . . ."

The difficulty with the inference we have made is that
it is not an instance of any valid rule of modal logic.
P is perhaps an instance of Q.

> *Q. If for every member of a set it is possible that it
> has a certain property then it is possible that
> every member of that set has that property.*

But Q is an invalid principle, as the following instantia-
tions of it make clear:

> *If for every member of the set of contingent propo-
> sitions it is possible that it is true then it is possible
> that every member of the set of contingent proposi-
> tions is true.*
>
> *If for every member of the set of candidates for
> President it is possible that he is elected President
> in 1976 then it is possible that every member of the
> set of candidates for President is elected President
> in 1976.*

It seems, then, that we cannot hope to justify P by appealing to the rules of logic. Of course, P might be necessarily true (for all we know) even though it is not an instance of a valid principle of modal logic. But how can we establish that the inference expressed by P is a correct inference? Before we try to answer this question, we need to see its importance for the Cosmological Argument.

The existence of the set of dependent beings will have an explanation just in case (i) there is an explanation of the existence of each of the members, and (ii) there is an explanation of why the set has members rather than not. On the supposition that every being is dependent, the explanation of why the set has members rather than not cannot be found in some being outside the set. Can it, then, be found within the set itself? How could the explanation of why a set has members be found within the set itself? Well, suppose a given set has a member whose existence is necessary rather than contingent. If so, then the reason why the set has members rather than not having any is that one of its members is such that it could not possibly not exist. In short, if there is a member of a given set whose existence is necessary then there is a reason why the set has members rather than not having any. Thus if we assume that God necessarily exists, then the explanation of why the set of existing beings has members rather than not would be found within the set itself, namely, in the being that necessarily exists.

Since no member of the infinite set of dependent beings is necessary, Clarke concludes that the explanation of why the set has members rather than not cannot be found within the set itself. But this conclusion is unwarranted if the inference now in question is incorrect. For suppose that, even though no dependent being necessarily exists, it is nevertheless necessary that some dependent beings exist. That is, suppose that the set in question is such that although no one of its members necessarily exists, it is necessary that the set has members. In this case too, it would seem, there is an explanation of why the set has members. It has members (at least one) because the set is such that it is logically impossible for it not to have members.

Clarke's position is that there is one, *and only one*, way in which A, the set of dependent beings, could have the explanation of its existence *within itself*. A would have the explanation of its existence within itself only if (i) each member of A has an explanation of its existence, and (ii) there is a member of A that necessarily exists. Condition (i), of course, obtains in A, the set of dependent beings. Each member has the explanation of its existence in the causal efficacy of some other being. Condition (ii), however, cannot obtain. For no being that has the reason for its existence in some other dependent being can be, in Clarke's words, "self-existent or necessarily existing." But there is, I think, a second way in which A, the set of dependent beings, could have the explanation of its existence within itself. A would have the explanation of its existence within itself if (i) each member of A has an explanation of its existence, and (iii) it is necessary that there exists at least one member of A. It is clear why Clarke did not consider this second way. He thought that, if condition (ii) did not obtain, then condition (iii) could not obtain. That is, Clarke thought that from the proposition

a. *Every member of A is such that it is possible that it does not exist (i.e., it is not the case that there is a member of A that necessarily exists).*

it follows that

163

b. It is possible that every member of A does not exist (i.e., it is not the case that it is necessary that there exists at least one member of A).

But the inference from (a) to (b) is precisely the inference in question. For, as we saw above, the rules of logic do not sanction this inference.

The importance of this inference for the Cosmological Argument should now be clear. If Clarke is wrong about this inference then, even though no being necessarily exists, it might be true (for all we know) that the set of dependent beings has the explanation of its existence within itself. For suppose that there are two members of A (d_1 and d_2) such that although it is possible that d_1 does not exist and possible that d_2 does not exist, it is *not possible* that both d_1 does not exist and d_2 does not exist. If this were so, then condition (iii) would obtain, i.e., it would be necessary that there exists at least one member of the set of dependent beings.

We know, for example, that, although no member of the set of contingent propositions is necessarily true, it is, nevertheless, necessary that some member of the set of contingent propositions is true. We know that although no horse in a given horse race necessarily will be the winner it is, nevertheless, necessary that some horse in the race will be the winner. Can we be sure that the set of dependent beings is not such that although no dependent being necessarily exists it is, nevertheless, necessary that some dependent being exists?

We noted above three conditions that are relevant to the question of whether the explanation of the existence of the collection of dependent beings is to be found within the collection itself. They are:

i. Each member of the collection has an explanation of its existence.

ii. *There is a member of the collection that neces-*
sarily exists.

iii. *It is necessary that there exists at least one*
member of the collection.

Hume thought that, from the truth of (i) *alone*, it follows that the existence of the collection of dependent
beings has an explanation. In support of Leibniz and
Clarke, I have argued that Hume was mistaken. Clarke
thought that from the assumption that every being is
dependent and the falsity of (ii) it follows that the existence of the collection of dependent beings has no explanation. I have argued that if (i) and (iii) are true
then, whether or not (ii) is true, the existence of the
infinite collection does have an explanation. Since the
proponent of the Cosmological Argument must show
that, on the assumption that every being is dependent,
the collection of dependent beings has *no explanation*,
it is clear that he must show that condition (iii) cannot
obtain. He must show that it is logically possible that
no dependent beings exist. Clarke's procedure, as I have
indicated, is to *infer* the proposition "It is logically possible that no dependent beings exist" from the obviously true proposition "Every dependent being is such that
it is logically possible that it does not exist." The difficulty is that this inference cannot be justified by appeal
to the rules of logic. Are we then left with an unjustified
assumption in the Cosmological Argument; namely,
that it is possible that no dependent beings exist—an
assumption without which the proponent of the Cosmological Argument cannot establish that the whole of
existing things does not consist of an infinite collection
of dependent beings?

Earlier I suggested that we concede to the proponent
of the Cosmological Argument the proposition that it is

logically possible that God exists. Given this proposition, perhaps it can be established that it is possible that no dependent beings exist.

> *1. It is necessary that if God exists then it is possible that there are no dependent beings.*
>
> *2. It is possible that God exists.*

Therefore:

> *3. It is possible that it is possible that there are no dependent beings.*

Therefore:

> *4. It is possible that there are no dependent beings.*

This argument consists of two premises, propositions (1) and (2), and two inferences. The first inference is from (1) and (2) to (3) and is obviously valid. The second inference, from (3) to (4), follows in accordance with the modal principle that if it is possible that a proposition is possible then that proposition is possible. Since the argument is valid and we have conceded premise (2), the only question at issue is premise (1).

It is, I think, a necessary truth—by virtue of the concept of God—that if God exists, then whether or not there are to be any dependent beings is wholly up to God. But if it is necessarily true that there are dependent beings, then the issue of whether or not there are to be dependent beings is not wholly up to God. Hence, the existence of God *entails* that it is possible that there are no dependent beings. Premise (1), therefore, is true.

In this chapter I have examined the two major criticisms advanced against that part of the Cosmological Argument that seeks to establish that not every being can be a dependent being. I have argued that each of these criticisms rests on a philosophical mistake and, therefore, fails as a refutation of the Cosmological Argument. If my arguments are correct, it does not follow, of course, that the Cosmological Argument is a good argument for its conclusion. But it does follow that those philosophers who have rejected the argument on the basis of either of the two criticisms discussed in this chapter need to reexamine the argument and, if they continue to reject it, provide some *good* reasons for doing so.

IV

The Cosmological Argument and the Idea of a Necessary Being

WE have been examining the first two steps in Clarke's argument for the existence of a necessary being. Before we consider the third and final step, it will be instructive here to distill from the preceding discussion what seems to be the essence of Clarke's Cosmological Argument.

It is helpful up to a point to develop the Cosmological Argument step-by-step as Clarke does: namely, first proving that at least one independent being has existed from eternity, etc. But it is not necessary to proceed in this step-by-step fashion. Indeed, having followed Clarke closely through the first two steps, it is now, I think, desirable to simplify his step-by-step argument by reconstructing it as a single piece of deductive reasoning for the conclusion that there exists a necessary being. If we use the expression "dependent being" to mean "a being that has the reason for its existence in the causal efficacy of some other beings," and the expression "independent being" to mean "a being that has the reason for its existence within its own nature," we may express the first part of the Cosmological Argument as follows:

1. *Every being is either a dependent being or an independent being.*
2. *It is false that every being is dependent.*

Therefore:

3. There exists an independent being.

Therefore:

4. There exists a necessary being.

This argument consists of two premises—propositions (1) and (2)—and two inferences, the inference from (1) and (2) to (3) and the inference from (3) to (4). Since the first of the two inferences is obviously valid, we are left with three points that require critical investigation—proposition (1), proposition (2), and the inference from proposition (3) to proposition (4). Proposition (1) expresses what we earlier called the strong form of PSR and represents the key principle in step one of Clarke's development of the Cosmological Argument. Proposition (2) and the reasoning that supports it represent step two in Clarke's development of the argument. Finally, the inference from (3) to (4) is the key move in step three of Clarke's argument. This inference is the portion of the argument that remains to be examined. A number of issues need to be examined in connection with the inference from (3) to (4). It is best, I believe, to begin with a consideration of the question: "What is meant by the expression *a necessary being?*"

Philosophers and theologians have used the expression *necessary being* in at least three different senses. In elucidating these three senses it will be helpful to refer to them by three different adjectives qualifying the expression *necessary being*: "factually necessary being," "causally necessary being," and "logically necessary being."[1]

[1] In an excellent study, "Necessary Being," *Scottish Journal of Theology* (December 1961), pp. 353-369, John Hick distinguishes

A being is *factually necessary* just in case (i) it is not causally dependent on any other being, and (ii) every other being is causally dependent on it. This is the weakest of the three senses of "necessary being" I shall distinguish. Some philosophers have contended that this is the sense of "necessary being" that is crucial to theism. Thus, Penelhum remarks:

> As applied to things or events, 'contingent' will mean 'dependent' or 'caused,' one thing or event being contingent *upon* another; 'necessary' will mean 'not dependent on any other,' and in addition, 'having others dependent on it.' A thing is necessary if it is indispensable. For want of a better phrase I shall call necessity in this sense 'factual necessity.' To be a theist is to believe that there is a being, God, who is factually necessary, all other beings being dependent, contingent upon him.[2]

Penelhum is undoubtedly right in maintaining that the theistic concept of God is such that God, if He exists, is a factually necessary being. It may be, however, that the theistic concept of God requires that God be necessary in some sense stronger than factually necessary. That is, while it is undoubtedly true that theism requires that God is a factually necessary being, it may be that theism also requires that God is either causally necessary or logically necessary. Be this as it may, the issue before us

---

two main senses: *factual necessity* and *logical necessity*. He thinks of *causal necessity* as a species of *factual necessity*. Indeed, what he describes as a factually necessary being comes very close to what I describe as a causally necessary being. What I describe as a factually necessary being is, I think, not recognized by Hick as a distinct sense of the phrase "a necessary being."

[2] Terrence Penelhum, "Divine Necessity," *Mind* (April 1960), p. 185.

is not what sort of necessary being is required by theism but what sort of necessary being is required by the Cosmological Argument. Hence, after distinguishing the three senses of "necessary being" we need to determine which, if any, is the sense employed in proposition (4) "There exists a necessary being."

A causally necessary being, like a factually necessary being, is such that every other being is causally dependent on it while it is causally independent of every other being. As opposed to a *merely* factually necessary being, however, a causally necessary being is such that it is *logically impossible* for it to be causally dependent on any other being and *logically impossible* for any other being to be causally independent of it. Plantinga argues that the theistic concept of God is such that God, if He exists, is a causally necessary being.

> Essential to theism is an assertion to the effect that there is a connection between God and all other beings, a connection in virtue of which others are causally dependent upon God. And this proposition is analytic; it is part of the Hebraic-Christian concept of God that He is "Maker of heaven and earth." But it is also a necessary truth that if God exists, He is Himself uncreated and in no way causally dependent upon anything else.[3]

Perhaps the distinction between a factually necessary being and a causally necessary being can be made clearer in terms of the theistic concept of God. Consider the following statement:

A. God is causally dependent on some other being or there exists a being that is causally independent of God.

[3] Alvin Plantinga, "Necessary Being" in A. Plantinga, ed., *Faith and Philosophy* (Grand Rapids, 1963), p. 107.

Now to assert that God is a *factually* necessary being is to assert that God exists and that (A) is false. To assert that God is a *causally* necessary being is to assert that God exists and that (A) is *necessarily* false. Thus, anyone who asserts that God is a causally necessary being implies that God is a factually necessary being. But the converse is not so. That is, in asserting that God is a factually necessary being, one does not imply that God is a causally necessary being. And this for the simple reason that to assert that a proposition is false—in this case (A)—is not to imply that it is *necessarily* false.

From the above, it appears that the way in which we determine whether a given being is such that it is logically impossible for it to be causally dependent on any other being and logically impossible for any other being to be causally independent of it is by determining whether a certain proposition about that being (e.g., (A) in the case of God) is *necessarily* false. But there would seem to be a difficulty in this procedure. For whether the proposition in question is necessarily false seems to depend on how we *specify* the being in question. For example, since the object of Eckhart's contemplation is identical with God, we may consider the proposition:

> B. *The object of Eckhart's contemplation is causally dependent on some other being or there exists a being that is causally independent of the object of Eckhart's contemplation.*

Now (B), like (A), is false. But, unlike (A), (B) is not necessarily false. For it is a contingent fact the Meister Eckhart spent his time contemplating God rather than, say, a stone. Since it is logically possible that the object of Eckhart's contemplation is a stone, it is logically possible that (B) is true. Hence, (B) is not necessarily false. Are we to conclude from this that although God is a causally necessary being, the object of Meister Eckhart's contemplation is not a causally necessary being? Clearly not. For since the object of Eckhart's contemplation *is* God, we would be implying that one and the same being both is and is not a causally necessary being. It appears that we need to amend the procedure by which we determine whether a being is or is not a causally necessary being.

The amendment I propose derives from a distinction Aquinas makes in remarking on the statement: "It is possible for a white thing to be black." Of this statement Thomas says, "it is false as applied to the saying, and true as applied to the thing; for a thing which is white can become black; whereas this saying, *a white thing is black*, can never be true."[4] Thomas is here distinguishing between taking the statement as an assertion that a certain white *thing* is possibly black, a *de re* modal statement, and taking the statement as an assertion that a certain *statement* is possible (i.e., possibly true), a *de dicto* modal statement. If taken *de re*, the statement is:

> *a. This white thing is possibly black.*

If taken *de dicto*, the statement is:

> *b. The statement "This white thing is black" is possible.*

(a), Thomas reminds us, is true. For the thing that in fact is white might have been black; its whiteness is not necessary to its being the thing it is. (b), however, is plainly false.

Aquinas has given us an example of a statement that

[4] ST, Q. 14, Art. 3, ad. 3.

is true *de re* but false *de dicto*. An example of a statement that is false *de re* but true *de dicto* is the following: "It is possible for the number of planets to be greater than 10." Taken *de re*, this statement is:

> c. *The number of planets is possibly greater than 10.*

Taken *de dicto*, this statement is:

> d. *The statement "The number of planets is greater than 10" is possible.*

Returning to our procedure, I shall say that it is logically impossible for x to be causally dependent on any other being if the *de re* statement that x is *possibly* causally dependent on some other being is false. Thus, it is logically impossible for God to be causally dependent on any other being if the statement

> e. *God is possibly causally dependent on some other being.*

is false. I shall say that it is logically impossible for any other being to be causally independent of x if the *de re* statement that x is possibly not causally necessary for every other being is false. Thus, it is logically impossible for any other being to be causally independent of God if the statement

> f. *God is possibly not causally necessary for every other being.*

is false.

The difficulty with our earlier procedure for determining whether x is causally necessary was that it seemed to depend on how we *specified* x. Thus when we employed the specification "God" we got one answer, and when we employed the specification "The object of Eckhart's contemplation" we got a different answer. This difficulty has now vanished. For if (e) is false, so is

g. *The object of Eckhart's contemplation is possibly causally dependent on some other being.*

And if (f) is false, so is

h. *The object of Eckhart's contemplation is possibly not causally necessary for every other being.*

For God is identical with the object of Eckhart's contemplation. In short, it will not now matter how we specify *x*. The specification of *x* makes a difference when a modal statement is taken *de dicto* but not when it is taken *de re*.[5]

In the course of developing what I have called the idea of a causally necessary being, Plantinga argues that the theistic concept of God is such that it is *causally impossible* for God to begin to exist and *causally impossible* for God (if He exists) to cease existing. Plantinga develops his argument as follows:

> God is a causally necessary condition of the existence of anything else, whereas His existence has no necessary conditions. Now the absence of a necessary condition of the existence of anything is a sufficient condition of the non-existence of that thing; and if a being has no

---

[5] It will be objected that we have escaped one difficulty only to fall into another. For a number of philosophers contend that no coherent account can be given either of *de re* modal statements or of the traditional view that among the properties of a thing some are essential, others merely accidental. This objection raises issues too complex and far-reaching to be investigated here. For an account of some of these issues see Alvin Plantinga, "De Re Et De Dicto," *Nous*, Vol. III, No. 3 (1969), pp. 235-258.

causally necessary conditions, then its non-existence has no causally sufficient conditions. And hence if God does exist, His going out of existence could have no causally sufficient conditions and is therefore impossible. If God has no necessary conditions, then it is analytic that His going out of existence, if it occurred, would be an uncaused event; for it is analytic that there can be no causally sufficient conditions of its occurrence. Similarly, His beginning to exist is causally impossible, for since it is analytic that God is not dependent upon anything, He has no cause; and hence His coming into existence would be an event which could have no causally sufficient conditions. So if God does exist, He cannot cease to exist; nor could He have begun to exist.[6]

There is, I think, a mistake in this argument. Compare the following two principles:

I. *If there are no causal conditions sufficient to bring about the non-existence of* x, *it is causally impossible for* x *to cease existing.*

II. *If there are causal conditions sufficient to bring about the continued existence of* x, *it is causally impossible for* x *to cease existing.*

Principle II is true. But it is far from clear that I is true. From the premise that it is causally possible for a certain event to occur, it does seem to follow that there are no causal conditions sufficient for its non-occurrence. This is precisely what II, when generalized, implies. But from the premise that it is causally possible for a certain event to occur it does not follow that there

[6] "Necessary Being," p. 107.

actually are causal conditions sufficient for it to occur. Hence, I is false. And it appears that some such principle as I is employed by Plantinga when he claims, "And hence if God does exist, His going out of existence could have no causally sufficient conditions and is therefore causally impossible." It matters not that it is logically impossible for there to exist conditions causally sufficient to bring about God's non-existence. All that follows from this is that it is necessarily true that if God exists His continued existence is causally possible, i.e., not causally impossible.

The point I have been laboring is simply that for an event or state of affairs p to be causally impossible it must be that causally sufficient conditions for non-p exist. Thus if God exists His non-existence is causally impossible only if there exist causally sufficient conditions for His continued existence. It is not enough that there exist no causally sufficient conditions for His non-existence. Indeed, I should think that in the case of God it would be necessarily true that, if He exists, neither His continued existence nor His ceasing to exist is *causally impossible*—there being no conditions causally sufficient for His continuing in existence or for His ceasing to exist.

Similarly, if God exists, we cannot conclude, as Plantinga does, that God's beginning to exist is causally impossible simply because there are no causally sufficient conditions for His coming into existence. God's beginning to exist is causally impossible only if there exist causally sufficient conditions to prevent His coming into existence. Again, I should think that in the case of God it would be necessarily true that, if He exists, neither His having begun to exist nor His not having begun to exist was causally impossible—there having been no conditions causally sufficient to bring Him into existence or to prevent His coming into existence.

What follows from all this is that neither God's existence nor His non-existence is causally impossible. For there can be no causally sufficient conditions for God's existence or for His non-existence. Necessarily then, if God exists, His existence is uncaused, and, if God does not exist, His non-existence is uncaused.

Plantinga concludes from this last point that the question "Why does God exist?" is an absurdity, a nonsensical question.

> Now it becomes clear that it is absurd to ask why God exists. To ask that question is to presuppose that God does exist; but it is a necessary truth that if He does, He has no cause. And it is also a necessary truth that if He has no cause, then there is no answer to a question asking for his causal conditions. The question "Why does God exist?" is, therefore, an absurdity.[7]

The unexpressed but crucial premise in this passage is that a question of the form "Why does x exist?" is an absurdity if it is not possible for there to be causally sufficient conditions for the existence of x. Since, as we have seen, it is not possible for there to be causally sufficient conditions for the existence of God, it follows— given Plantinga's unexpressed but crucial premise— that the question "Why does God exist?" is absurd.

Whatever else we may think about Plantinga's premise, it is clear that it is *incompatible* with the strong form of PSR. For that principle implies that for every being, including God, there is an answer to the question

[7] *Ibid.*

"Why does it exist?" PSR (the strong form) asserts that every being has an explanation of its existence. Of course, PSR is not incompatible with the view that some being is such that there is and can be no answer to a question asking for its causal conditions. Indeed, in the context of the Cosmological Argument, the principle is used to show that there exists such a being. The issue, then, between Plantinga's premise and PSR has to do with what can count as an answer to the question "Why does this thing exist?" Plantinga's argument presupposes that the proposition "There is an answer to the question of why x exists" entails the proposition "There are causally sufficient conditions for the existence of x." PSR in its strong form implies that there is an answer to the question "Why does x exist?" even though there are no conditions that caused x to exist. For the principle implies that the answer to the question "Why does x exist?" may be found within the *nature* of x, in which case there would be no other being or conditions that caused x to exist. Therefore, granting Plantinga's point that it is logically impossible for God's existence to be caused, what follows from the strong form of PSR is that God, if He exists, has the reason of His existence within His own nature. Thus, if God exists and PSR is true, the answer to the question "Why does God exist?" is to be found within God's own nature.

In a later work, Plantinga claims that the question "Why does God exist?" never does in fact arise. It does not arise because it is a request for causal conditions and, therefore, is a senseless question.[8] But the question of why God exists rather than not surely does arise in

[8] *God and Other Minds* (Ithaca, New York: Cornell University Press, 1967), p. 182.

179

the reflections of a number of classical theologians and philosophers. And the answer given is not in terms of causal conditions but in terms such as "because His essence is identical with His existence" (Aquinas) or "because He carries the reason of His existence within His nature" (Samuel Clarke).

Indeed, those theologians and philosophers who accepted PSR certainly thought that the question "Why does God exist?" is a sensible question. For as we have noted, according to that principle, whatever exists has an explanation of its existence—either in the causal efficacy of some other being or in the necessity of its own nature. Of course, Plantinga is correct in claiming that the theistic conception of God is such that *if* the question "Why does God exist?" is construed as a question asking for God's causal conditions, then that question is senseless. But the question "Why does God exist rather than not?" is not, I think, so construed by a number of philosophers and theologians. And it is far from clear that a well-developed theism can rest content with a conception of God as necessary only in the sense of a causally necessary being.

Thus far I have tried to distinguish and clarify two different senses in which philosophers have used the phrase "a necessary being"—namely, a *factually* necessary being and a *causally* necessary being. The third sense in which the phrase has been used is expressed by the idea of a *logically* necessary being. Although this sense needs to be considered in detail, for the moment it must suffice to characterize a logically necessary being as a being whose non-existence is a logical impossibility. Some philosophers—notably Anselm, Descartes, and Leibniz—have held that God is a necessary being in the sense of a *logically* necessary being. That is, they have held that the non-existence of God is a logical impossibility.

It is important to observe that the proposition "God is a causally necessary being" does not entail the proposition "God is a logically necessary being." If God is a causally necessary being, then it is logically impossible for some other being to be a causally necessary condition of God's existence. But this does not imply that God's non-existence is logically impossible.

Which, if any, of the three senses of "necessary being" is employed in the conclusion of part I of the Cosmological Argument? That is, which sense is employed in proposition (4) "There exists a necessary being?" Proposition (4) is, as I have represented the Cosmological Argument, inferred from proposition (3) "There exists an independent being." An examination of the reasoning Clarke employs in moving from the existence of an independent being to the existence of a necessary being will provide the answer to our question.

After establishing that an independent being exists, Clarke argues that the independent being must be *self-existent*.

> For whatever exists must either have come into being out of nothing, absolutely without cause; or it must have been produced by some external cause; or it must be self-existent. Now to arise out of nothing, absolutely without any cause; has been already shown to be a plain contradiction. To have been produced by some external cause, cannot possibly be true of every thing; but something must have existed eternally and independently; as has likewise been shown already. It remains therefore, that the being which has existed independently from eternity, must of necessity be self-existent (*Demonstration*, p. 15).

By a "self-existent" being, Clarke does not simply mean an eternal being that does not exist by the causal activity of some other beings. Nor, of course, does he mean a being that brings itself into existence. He means what I have built into the meaning of the expression "an independent being," namely, a being that has the reason of its existence within its own nature. He explains self-existence as follows:

> Now to be self-existent, is not, to be produced by itself; for that is an express contradiction. But it is, (which is the only idea we can frame of self-existence; and without which, the word seems to have no signification at all). It is, I say, to exist by an absolute necessity originally in the nature of the thing itself (*Demonstration*, p. 15).

The question that remains is whether a self-existent or independent being is a being whose non-existence is a *logical* impossibility. That Clarke does intend this to follow from the idea of a self-existent being, is, I think, clear from the following:

> . . . that the only true idea of a self-existent or necessarily existing being, is the idea of a being the supposition of whose non-existing is an express contradiction. For since it is absolutely impossible but there must be somewhat self-existent; that is, which exists by the necessity of its own nature; it is plain that that necessity cannot be a necessity consequent upon any foregoing supposition, (because nothing can be antecedent to that which is self-existence,) but it must be a necessity absolutely such in its own nature. Now a necessity, not relatively or consequentially, but absolutely such in its own nature; is nothing else, but its being a plain impossi-

bility or implying a contradiction to suppose the contrary. For instance: the relation of equality between twice two and four, is an absolute necessity; only because it is an immediate contradiction in terms to suppose them unequal. This is the only idea we can frame, of an absolute necessity; and to use the word in any other sense, seems to be using it without any signification at all (*Demonstration*, p. 17).

This passage leaves no question as to which of the three senses of "a necessary being" Clarke is using when he claims that there exists a necessary being. He means, of course, that there exists a *logically* necessary being, i.e., a being whose non-existence is logically impossible.

Before considering the philosophical objections to the idea of a logically necessary being, we need to get Clarke's view as clear as possible. As we noted above, Clarke maintains that there must be a reason why a thing exists rather than not (the strong form of PSR). If the reason why a thing exists does not lie in the causal efficacy of some other being then the reason must lie within the thing itself. Clarke's clearest statement of this principle occurs in a letter replying to a critic. "Of everything that is, there is a reason which now does, or once or always did, determine the existence rather than the non-existence of that thing. Of that which derives not its being from any other thing, this reason or ground of existence, (whether we can attain to any *idea* of it, or no) must lie in the thing itself" (*Demonstration*, p. 489). The difficulty, of course, is to make sense of the view that the reason why a thing exists rather than not can lie within the thing itself.

One notable attempt at explaining how a thing may have the reason of its existence within itself is developed in the Ontological Argument, namely, in the idea that the nature or essence of a being *entails* the existence of that thing. Thus it is argued that a being whose nature is such that it includes every possible perfection is a being whose non-existence is logically impossible. For if it did not exist, it would not be what it is—a being whose nature includes every possible perfection. The *reason* then why God exists rather than not is to be found within His nature, and since His nature entails His existence, His having that nature explains why He exists rather than not. Perhaps if we examine Clarke's view of the Ontological Argument we can get a clearer idea of just what he thinks might constitute *the reason within the thing itself* why it exists rather than not.

If he does not decisively reject the Ontological Argument, Clarke does express considerable doubt about it.

> The argument which has by some been drawn from our including self-existence in the idea of God, or our comprehending it in the definition or notion we frame of him; has this obscurity and defect in it: that it seems to extend only to the nominal idea or mere definition of a self-existent being, and does not with a sufficiently evident connection refer and apply that general nominal idea, definition, or notion which we frame in our own mind, to any real particular being actually existing without us. For it is not satisfactory that I have in my mind an idea of the proposition; *there exists a being indued with all possible perfections*: or, *there is a self-existent being*. But I must also have some idea of the thing. I must have an idea of something actually existing without me. And I must see wherein consists the absolute impossibility of removing that idea, and consequently of supposing the non-existence of the thing;

before I can be satisfied from that idea, that the thing actually exists (*Demonstration*, pp. 20-21).

It is no easy matter to understand Clarke's view of the Ontological Argument. Suppose we define "God" as a self-existing, absolutely perfect being. Can we, after the fashion of the Ontological Argument, infer from this definition that God exists, i.e., that a self-existing, absolutely perfect being exists? Clarke, apparently, is saying that we *cannot*. For, Clarke seems to maintain, the existential proposition "God exists" will be true only if our idea of a self-existing, absolutely perfect being is an idea of "something actually existing without me." And, apparently, Clarke thinks that from the mere fact that we have the idea of a self-existing, absolutely perfect being it does not follow that our idea is an idea of something that actually exists.

As stated, this objection is not likely to impress the proponent of the Ontological Argument. Indeed, he is likely to claim that Clarke's own position is incoherent. Clarke seems to hold that the existential proposition "A self-existing, absolutely perfect being exists" is not just true but *necessarily* true. For if it were possible for this proposition to be false, then it would be possible that the idea of a self-existing, supremely perfect being is not the idea of something actually existing. And, as Clarke himself claims, "the only true idea of a self-existent or necessarily existing being, is the idea of a being, the supposition of whose non-existing is an express contradiction" (*Demonstration*, p. 17). But if the existential proposition "A self-existing, absolutely perfect being exists" is necessarily true, how could it be possible for us to have the idea of a self-existing, absolutely perfect being without it being true that our idea is an idea of an actually existing being?

Clarke, so far as I know, does not develop his objection to the Ontological Argument beyond these brief remarks. Nor does he indicate how he would respond to the claim that his own position is incoherent. At the risk of misinterpreting Clarke's view of the Ontological Argument, I propose to develop his objection to the argument. For it seems that his objection contains an important point that is missed in the standard objections to the argument.

Consider the following simple version of the Ontological Argument:

> *A. 1. "God" = df. an existing, absolutely perfect being.*
>
> > *2. It is not possible that an existing, absolutely perfect being does not exist.*
>
> *Therefore:*
>
> > *3. It is not possible that God does not exist.*

There are two traditional objections to this argument. The major objection, made famous by Kant, is that existence is not a real predicate and, therefore, cannot be a part of the definition of a concept. This objection rejects the first premise of our argument (A). The second objection—an objection Leibniz formulated and endeavored to answer—is to the idea of an absolutely perfect being. It holds that this idea is internally incoherent, like the idea of a supremely large number. It is clear that neither of these well-known objections is the objection advanced by Clarke. What then is Clarke's objection? (Or perhaps more accurately, what is the objection that I think is being suggested by Clarke's critical remarks?)

Clarke's objection is that by simply *defining* the term "God" so as to include *existence* in the definition we cannot directly infer that God exists. Now this is not Kant's objection. Clarke is not saying that we cannot have a definition of a term that includes existence as one of the predicates in the definition. He is not saying that existence is not a predicate. What he is saying is that, from that definition, we cannot infer the *existential proposition* that God exists.

As applied to our simplified version of the Ontological Argument, it would seem that Clarke's objection must be either to the second premise or to the derivation of the conclusion from the premises. For, unlike Kant, he appears to grant the procedure that yields the first premise. But what could be wrong with either the second premise or the derivation of (3) from (1) and (2)?

(3) follows from (2) and (1) by the standard principle of substituting the definiendum ("God") for the definiens ("an existing, absolutely perfect being"). And the proposition "An existing, absolutely perfect being does not exist" seems to be a contradiction—hence, (2) appears to be true.

Consider the following argument:

B. *1. "A vetinling"* = *df. an existing doctor who cares for animals and speaks their language.*

　2. It is not possible that an existing doctor who cares for animals and speaks their language does not exist.

Therefore:

　3. It is not possible that a vetinling does not exist.

No one is likely to be persuaded by this argument that there actually exists—let alone, necessarily exists—a doctor who cares for animals and speaks their language. But what is wrong with this argument? I suggest that its conclusion (3) is *ambiguous* between

> *3a. It is not possible that any non-existing thing is a vetinling,*

and

> *3b. It is not possible that no existing thing is a vetinling.*

(3b) entails an existential proposition, namely, that there exists at least one vetinling. (3a), however, does not have this entailment. From (3a) we learn only that no non-existing thing can be a vetinling. If we construe (3) as ambiguous between the non-existential proposition (3a) and the existential proposition (3b), what follows concerning our evaluation of (B)?

Our evaluation of (B) is complicated by the fact that insofar as there is an ambiguity in (3), a similar ambiguity affects (2). For (2) may be construed as

> *2a. It is not possible that any non-existing thing is an existing doctor who cares for animals and speaks their language*

or as

> *2b. It is not possible that no existing thing is an existing doctor who cares for animals and speaks their language.*

The ambiguity in (3) and (2) allows us to construct from (B) four distinct arguments, of which the following three are of interest:

> *B1. The argument from (1) and (2a) to (3b).*
> *B2. The argument from (1) and (2b) to (3b).*
> *B3. The argument from (1) and (2a) to (3a).*

It is clear that, if (2) is construed as the non-existential (2a), and (3) is construed as the existential proposition (3b), then the argument, i.e., (B1), is *invalid*. On the other hand, if we endeavor to make the inference to the existential conclusion (3b) valid by construing (2) as (2b), as in argument (B2), we purchase *validity* at the price of introducing the false premise (2b). Since there are no *existing* doctors who speak the language of animals (assuming that animals have a language) and since (2b) entails that there do exist such doctors, (2b) is false.

What we have just seen is that if argument (B) is construed as an "ontological" argument, an argument that contains an existential proposition as its conclusion, i.e. (3b), the argument will either be *invalid*, i.e. (B1), or contain a *false* premise, i.e. (B2), depending on whether we interpret its second premise as the *true*, but *non-existential* proposition (2a) or as the *existential*, but *false* proposition (2b). In either case, the argument is seen to be unsuccessful as an argument for the existential proposition (3b).

If we take (3) as the non-existential proposition (3a), however, the argument, i.e. (B3), is a *sound* argument for its conclusion. Its conclusion, it must be admitted, is not very significant. What it tells us is that the concept of a vetinling necessarily is not exhibited by any non-existing thing. Given that the definition of "vetinling" includes the predicate *existence*, this, of course, should come as no surprise.

It might be thought that what we are told by the conclusion (3a)—i.e., that the concept of a vetinling is inapplicable to any non-existing thing—is altogether trivial in that no concept applies to (or is exhibited by) any thing unless that thing does *exist*. But it is doubtful that this is so. Consider, for example, the following definition:

*"A vetinlang" = df. A doctor who cares for animals
and speaks their language.*

So far as I know no existing thing is a vetinlang. But
at least one non-existing thing—in this case a fictional
being—is a vetinlang: namely, Dr. Doolittle. Why cannot Dr. Doolittle exhibit a concept? We can talk about
Dr. Doolittle, have an actor portray him, refer to him,
etc. Why cannot we apply a concept to him or say that
he exhibits a concept? At any rate, *if* Dr. Doolittle does
exhibit certain concepts, our argument (B3) is not altogether trivial. For it establishes not that there exists a
vetinling but that Dr. Doolittle (and any other *non-
existing* doctor who cares for and speaks the language
of animals) is not a vetinling.

Before applying these considerations to our simplified
version of the Ontological Argument, it is perhaps
worth noting that we may define a term so as to include
non-existence in its definition, thus providing the basis
for an "ontological" argument of the non-existence of
a thing. For example, consider the argument:

> *C. 1. "A magico" = df. A non-existing magician.*
>
>   *2. It is not possible that a non-existing magi-
> cian exists.*

Therefore:

> *3. It is not possible that a magico exists.*

Following our earlier suggestion concerning the ambiguity of certain statements, we may construe (3) in (C) as

> *3a. It is not possible that any existing thing is a
> magico.*

or as

> *3b. It is not possible that no non-existing thing is a magico.*

(A similar ambiguity is present in (2).) It should be clear that insofar as we construe (C) to be a *sound* argument, what it establishes is (3a), not (3b). Given (3a) as established, we may conclude, for example, that neither Houdini nor the Great Blackstone is a magico. Merlin, however, is a magico. If we define "A magican" as an *existing* magician, both Houdini and the Great Blackstone will be magicans, but not Merlin. The term "magician," however, applies indifferently to magicos and magicans.

The application of these considerations to our simplified version of the Ontological Argument (A) should now be clear. What the argument establishes is

> *3a. It is not possible that any non-existing being is God.*

and not

> *3b. It is not possible that no existing being is God.*

For if we construe the conclusion of the argument as the existential proposition (3b), the argument will be invalid or contain the suspicious premise

> *2b. It is not possible that no existing being is an existing, absolutely perfect being.*

I say that (2b) is *suspect* since our Ontological Argument provides us with no grounds for thinking that it is true.

I have been arguing that the result of including *existence* among the predicates in the definition of a term is to exclude all non-existing things from the class of things to which the term may apply, and not to guarantee that there is some thing to which the term applies. If this is correct, then even though we include *existence* as one of the predicates in our definition of "God," we cannot conclude that God exists until we establish that there actually exists something to which the definition of "God" (or to which our *idea* of God) applies. And this seems to be the point Clarke raises concerning the Ontological Argument. For he objects that it is not sufficient to have the idea of God as a *self-existent* being in order to conclude that God exists. "But I must also have some idea of the thing. I must have an idea of something actually existing without me. And I must see wherein consists the absolute impossibility of removing that idea, and consequently of supposing the non-existence of the thing; before I can be satisfied from that idea, that the thing actually exists" (*Demonstration*, p. 21).

It would be a mistake, however, to conclude that the objection I have sketched adequately reflects Clarke's view. For the objection I have presented suggests that even when a term in whose definition we have included *existence* does apply to something, the existence of that thing may be contingent, not necessary. Thus, for example, having defined "a magican" as an existing magician, we know that the term "magican" does apply to Houdini and the Great Blackstone, neither of which is a *necessary being*. Similarly, even if we should establish that the term "God," when defined as "an existing, absolutely perfect being," does apply to something, we would seem to have no grounds at all for regarding His existence as necessary rather than contingent. But surely, if this is the direction our objection leads, it cannot be an adequate reflection of Clarke's view. For Clarke holds that God is a necessary being, that if the concept "God" applies to something, then that thing's existence is logically necessary. His objection to the Ontological Argument is *not* that the idea of God is such that it might (for all we know) apply to something whose existence is contingent. Rather, his objection is that the argument does not establish that the idea of God applies at all. Clarke does not say that the Ontological Argument fails to establish that the idea of God is such that any thing to which that idea applies must be a being whose non-existence is logically impossible. What he thinks the Ontological Argument fails to establish is that the idea of God does apply to something (i.e., "is an idea of something actually existing without me"). But the objection I have sketched to the version of the Ontological Argument presented above seems to show that the argument not only fails to establish that the term "God" applies to something but also that the argument does not establish that the term "God" (as defined in the first premise) is such that any thing to which that idea applies must be a being whose non-existence is logically impossible.

Perhaps the difficulty just noted can be removed if we, following Clarke, include *self-existence* rather than *existence* in the definition of "God." As we know, Clarke distinguishes between a being that exists by reason of the causal efficacy of some other being and a being that exists "by an absolute necessity in the nature of the thing itself." Both exist, but only the latter has what Clarke calls "self-existence." Suppose, then, we adopt the following definition:

"a self-existing being" = *df. An existing being that
exists by reason of the
necessity of its nature.*

Using "self-existence" as just defined, we can clarify the
difference between *existence* and *self-existence* by considering the possible application of the term "magicani," when defined as follows:

"A magicani" = *df. A self-existing magician.*

Merlin, of course, cannot be a magicani. For necessarily
if *x* is a magicani then *x* is a magican (an existing magician). But Merlin, although he is a magician, is not a
magican. The Great Blackstone, however, although he
is a magican (an existing magician), is not a magicani
(a self-existing magician). Blackstone is not a magicani
because the supposition of his non-existence is not a
logical impossibility. Nothing about Blackstone's nature
renders his non-existence impossible.

Following Clarke, suppose we present the Ontological
Argument as follows:

1. *"God"* = *df. A self-existing, absolutely perfect
   being.*
2. *It is not possible that a self-existing, absolutely
   perfect being does not exist.*

Therefore:

3. *It is not possible that God does not exist.*

Clarke, as I have interpreted him, says of this argument
that it fails to establish the existence of God, that it
fails to show that the idea of God applies to something
actually existing. The objection I have sketched agrees
with this criticism. For on that objection, all that the

argument proves is the exclusion of various classes of things from the class of things to which the term "God" might apply. As does the version of the argument that begins with the definition of "God" as an existing, absolutely perfect being, this argument precludes *non-existing* things from membership in the class of things to which the term "God" may be applied. Again, like the former argument, this version excludes a certain class of existing things from inclusion in the class of things to which the term "God" may be applied; namely, the class that is the product of the class of existing things and the class of things that are not absolutely perfect. *Unlike* the former argument, however, this argument excludes a further class of existing things from the class of things to which the term "God" may be applied, namely, the class that is the product of the class of absolutely perfect beings and the class of existing things that do not exist by reason of the necessity of their natures. In short, this version of the Ontological Argument establishes—whereas the former does not—that no *contingently* existing being can be God.

Having removed the difficulty that prevented my objection from adequately reflecting Clarke's view of the Ontological Argument, we can now sum up what seem to be the main features of Clarke's position on the Ontological Argument. Clarke appears to hold:

1. *that the Ontological Argument fails to establish that the idea of God applies to some existing being,*
2. *that the Ontological Argument does establish that if the idea of God does apply to some existing being then that being to which it applies is such that its non-existence is logically impossible,*

195

3. *that what is needed is a proof that there does actually exist a being to which the idea of God applies,*

4. *that the Cosmological Argument (i.e., its first part) does establish that there exists a being that is self-existent, a being whose non-existence is logically impossible,*

and,

5. *that the Cosmological Argument (i.e., its second part) does establish that this self-existent being is absolutely perfect and, therefore, is such that the idea of God applies to it.*

One final point concerning Clarke's view of the Ontological Argument needs to be made clear. In summarizing Clarke's view, I said that he holds "that the Ontological Argument fails to establish that the idea of God applies to some existing being." This remark, however, is unclear. For on the one hand it could be taken to mean that Clarke holds that from the mere fact that we have the idea of God as a self-existing, absolutely perfect being *it does not follow* that this idea applies to some existing being. On this reading, Clarke's objection to the Ontological Argument would be a *logical* objection. On the other hand, the remark could be taken to mean that Clarke holds that from the mere fact that we have the idea of God as a self-existing, absolutely perfect being *we cannot know* whether this idea applies to some existing being. On this reading, Clarke's objection to the Ontological Argument would be an *epistemological* objection. Which of these two readings best reflects Clarke's position?

Although Clarke's own remarks about the Ontological Argument do not clearly indicate whether his objection is logical or epistemological, there is at least one reason why he should have held (if he did not) that the defect in the Ontological Argument is epistemological rather than logical. For Clarke certainly holds that the concept of God as a self-existent, absolutely perfect being is *necessarily* exemplified. That is, he holds that it is a *necessary truth* that there exists an absolutely perfect being. But since a necessary truth follows from any proposition whatever, Clarke cannot consistently hold the view that from the fact that we have the idea of God as a self-existing, perfect being it does not follow that this idea applies to some existing being.

Construing his objection to the Ontological Argument as epistemological, Clarke's point is that, by merely considering a certain concept or definition, we cannot be in a position to *know* that the concept or definition is exemplified by any existing thing. This point, however, does not imply either that the concept is not exemplified *or* that if it is exemplified it might (logically) not have been. Clarke's objection, then, is that by merely considering a concept all that we are in a position to *know* is that from the concept it follows that it is inapplicable to certain classes of being. It may, *for all we know*, be logically necessary for the concept to be exemplified. Clarke believes that it is logically necessary for the concept of a self-existent being to be exemplified. But he does not think that this belief can be *justified* by merely examining the concept of a self-existent being. The justification of the belief is the proof provided by the Cosmological Argument that there exists a necessary being.

We undertook an examination of Clarke's remarks concerning the Ontological Argument in the hope of getting clear what Clarke might mean by the phrase "the reason of a thing's existence being within the thing's own nature." Although we have learned (perhaps) how one can hold consistently both that God's existence is necessary and that certain versions of the Ontological Argument are defective, we have not uncovered in Clarke's remarks any explanation of what it is for a thing's nature to contain the explanation of its existence. The truth, I think, is that Clarke cannot tell us just what it is about a thing's nature that might explain its existence. All that Clarke claims to know is that there must exist at least one such being. And his reasons for this are now familiar. PSR entails that there is an explanation of the existence of every being. But not every being's existence can be explained by (the causal efficacy of) some other being. Therefore, some being must be such that the explanation of its existence is to be found within itself. These reasons, then, lead Clarke to the view that there exists a being such that the reason why it exists rather than not is within the thing's own nature. But the further question as to just *what* it is about that being's nature such that its nature explains its existence is a question Clarke is unable to answer.

The Cosmological Argument, as we have presented it, contains an inference from

3. *There exists an independent being (a being that has the reason for its existence within its own nature).*

to

4. *There exists a necessary being.*

We determined that, by the expression "necessary being" in (4), Clarke means a *logically* necessary being. But does (4) follow from (3)? In order to answer this question we sought to elucidate the crucial phrase in (3)—"a being that has the reason for its existence within its own nature." The Ontological Argument might be construed as providing such an explanation, for that argument purports to show that and how the existence of God is deducible from His nature. But as we saw, Clarke rejects the Ontological Argument and nowhere provides us with an explanation of the crucial phrase occurring in (3).

In spite of this fact, I do not think the meaning of the phrase in (3) is so obscure as to prevent us from evaluating the inference from (3) to (4). Indeed, I suspect that the reason why we find no explanation of its meaning in Clarke's work is that he did not think its meaning required explanation. Be that as it may, I think we can make sense of the phrase in question.

There are two sorts of facts about things. There are those facts about a thing that obtain simply because of the nature or essence of the thing in question and those facts about a thing that do not so obtain. The fact that Socrates taught Plato, for example, is a fact about Socrates that does not obtain simply because of the nature or essence of Socrates. Put somewhat differently, there are possible worlds in which Socrates exists with the nature or essence he has in this and every other world in which he exists but in which Socrates does not have the property of teaching Plato. Hence, the reason that the fact that Socrates taught Plato obtains is not simply because of the nature or essence of Socrates. The fact, however, that Socrates was a man obtains simply because of the nature or essence of Socrates. Put somewhat differently, there are no possible worlds in which Socrates exists with the nature or essence he has in this and every other world in which he exists but in which Socrates lacks the property of being a man.

The central idea to emerge from these considerations is that the reason why certain facts about a thing obtain may lie within the thing's nature or essence. To say that the thing's nature or essence is the *reason* why the fact in question obtains is simply to observe that the fact in question stands in a relation to the thing's nature or essence such that it is logically necessary that if the thing in question exists then the fact in question obtains. Socrates's nature or essence is such that it is logically necessary that if Socrates exists then the fact of his being a man obtains; whereas it is not logically necessary that if Socrates exists then the fact of his being a teacher of Plato obtains. The reason why Socrates is a man lies within his nature or essence; the reason why Socrates taught Plato does not lie within his nature or essence.

Putting aside the metaphysical problems associated with the idea of a thing's having a nature or essence, the above account gives content to the idea of a thing's nature or essence being the reason why a certain fact about that thing obtains. Suppose we now take the further step of viewing the existence of a thing as a fact *about* that thing. If we do take this further step, we can raise the question as to which sort of fact the existence of a thing is. Is it a fact that obtains simply because of the nature or essence of the thing in question, or is it a fact which does not so obtain? Clarke's view is that at least one being exists such that the fact that it exists is a fact of the first sort; that is, a fact that obtains simply because of the nature or essence of the being in question.

The Idea of a Necessary Being

Even if it is admitted that some facts about a thing may obtain simply because of the nature or essence of the thing in question, it will be objected that it is impossible for the fact that a thing exists to be such a fact. For, as we suggested earlier, a fact about a thing has this special relation to that thing's essence just in case it is logically necessary that if the thing in question exists then the fact in question obtains. And, of course, it is a trivial truth about anything whatever that if it exists then the fact that it exists obtains. Hence, everything, whether it exists or not, would be such that the reason for its existence lies within its nature or essence—and this is clearly absurd.

This objection can be avoided by the following qualification. In the case of any *non-existential* fact about an object, we shall say that the nature or essence of that object is the reason why that fact obtains provided that in every possible world in which that object exists the fact in question obtains. Since in every possible world in which Socrates exists, the fact that Socrates is a man obtains, Socrates's nature or essence is the reason why the fact that Socrates is a man obtains. In the case of an *existential* fact about an object, we shall say that the nature or essence of that object is the reason why that existential fact obtains provided that the existential fact in question obtains in every possible world.

The ordinary things with which we are acquainted are such that their existence is not explained in terms of their natures. For objects such as chairs, tables, cabbages and kings do not exist in every possible world. Their existence is explained by the causal efficacy of other beings. But if the Cosmological Argument is correct, there exists at least one being such that the reason for its existence—that is, the reason why the fact that it exists obtains—lies within its own nature or essence.

The account I have given of Clarke's phrase "the reason of a thing's existence being within its own nature" has the following consequence: the inference from

> 3. *There exists an independent being (a being that has the reason for its existence within its own nature).*

to

> 4. *There exists a necessary being.*

is thereby shown to be *valid*. For as we have seen, by "a necessary being" Clarke means a *logically* necessary being, a being whose non-existence is an absolute impossibility. But a being has the reason for its existence within its own nature only if it exists in every possible world. And clearly if any being exists in every possible world then that being is such that its non-existence is absolutely impossible. Hence, on the interpretation I have given of the crucial phrase in (3), the inference of (4) from (3) is valid.

The conclusion of the first part of the Cosmological Argument (proposition (4)) asserts the existence of a necessary being. As we noted earlier, many philosophers would be content to reject the Cosmological Argument for this reason alone. That is, they hold that there are good reasons for thinking that it is logically impossible for there to be a necessary being in the sense required by proposition (4). If they are correct, then there are good reasons for thinking that the Cosmological Argument is either invalid or contains a false premise. Hence, it is important here to examine the reasons that have been advanced against the idea of a logically necessary being.

Other philosophers have objected not to the idea of a logically necessary being *as such*, but to the Cosmological Argument's having as its conclusion the proposition that such a being exists. Some think that it is just a mistake to hold that the Cosmological Argument has as its conclusion the proposition that there exists a being whose existence is logically necessary. Others contend that if the conclusion asserts the existence of a logically necessary being then the conclusion could not be established by the premises of the argument. Before examining the reasons advanced against the idea of a logically necessary being, I shall discuss these two objections to the Cosmological Argument's having as its conclusion the claim that there exists a necessary being.

It has been argued that the conclusion of the Cosmological Argument asserts the existence of a necessary being in the sense of a being whose existence is uncaused, eternal, but not logically necessary.[9] This view is incorrect, since as we have seen, the version of the argument we are examining does have as its conclusion the claim that there exists a being whose existence is logically necessary. It is important, however, to recognize that some important versions of the argument—e.g., Aquinas's third way—do argue for the existence of a necessary being where the "necessity" in question is not logical necessity.[10] The truth of the matter is that the *kind* of necessity asserted in the conclusion—whether factual, causal, or logical—is not an essential feature of the Cos-

[9] Bruce Reichenbach has argued this in "Divine Necessity and The Cosmological Argument," *The Monist*, Vol. 54, No. 3, Part II (July 1970), pp. 401-415.

[10] See Patterson Brown, "St. Thomas' Doctrine of Necessary Being," *The Philosophical Review*, LXXIII, No. 1 (January 1964), pp. 76-90.

mological Argument. It is just as incorrect to claim that by "a necessary being" *the* Cosmological Argument means a logically necessary being,[11] as it is to claim that by "a necessary being" *the* Cosmological Argument means something other than a logically necessary being. Some important versions of the argument argue for the existence of a logically necessary being and others do not.

The second objection is that, if the conclusion of the argument is that there exists a *logically* necessary being, then the premises of the argument fail to establish that conclusion. To understand this objection, we need first to consider an important point concerning the proposition "There exists a logically necessary being." This proposition has the interesting characteristic that if it is true then it is necessarily true. "There exists a logically necessary being" cannot be a *contingent* truth. That this is so can be seen by the following *reductio ad absurdum* argument:

1. There exists a logically necessary being.

2. (1) is a contingent truth.

Therefore:

3. It is possible that it is false that there exists a being whose non-existence is logically impossible (from 2).

Therefore:

4. It is possible that every being is such that its non-existence is logically possible (from 3).

Therefore:

[11] J.J.C. Smart makes this erroneous claim in "The Existence of God" in A. Flew and Alasdair McIntyre, eds., *New Essays in Philosophical Theology* (New York: The Macmillan Company, 1955).

5. *Every being is such that it is possible that its non-existence is possible (from 4).*

Therefore:

6. *Every being is such that its non-existence is possible (from 5).*

7. *(6) contradicts (1).*

Therefore:

8. *(1) cannot be a contingent truth.*

Therefore:

9. *If (1) is true it is necessarily true.*[12]

The conclusion of the Cosmological Argument (i.e., the version we are considering) is such that, if it is true, it is a necessary truth. The objection I wish to consider can be expressed as follows. If the conclusion of the Cosmological Argument asserts the existence of a *logically* necessary being, then that conclusion is either false or necessarily true. If it is false, the argument cannot, of course, be a proof of its conclusion. On the other hand, if it is necessarily true then, again, the argument cannot be a proof of its conclusion. Hence, if the Cosmological Argument is to qualify as a *proof*, then its conclusion cannot be equivalent to the proposition "There exists a logically necessary being."

The difficulty with this objection is its contention

[12] If we symbolize the proposition "There exists a being whose non-existence is logically impossible" as $(\exists x)\sim P(x$ does not exist) then steps (3) to (6) proceed as follows:

3. $P\sim(\exists x)\sim P(x$ does not exist)
4. $P(x)P(x$ does not exist)
5. $(x)PP(x$ does not exist)
6. $(x)P(x$ does not exist)

Step (5) follows from (4) by the principle that $P(x) Fx \rightarrow (x)PFx$; and (6) follows from (5) by means of the principle that $PP \leftrightarrow P$.

that if the conclusion of the Cosmological Argument is a necessary truth then the argument cannot be a proof of its conclusion. Why should we accept this contention? Two reasons for accepting it have been advanced by William Kennick.[13] Where p represents the conjunction of premises of an argument and q represents its conclusion, Kennick argues that if q is *a priori* true then q is not a deductive consequence of p and p is not evidence for q. (By an *a priori* true proposition Kennick means a proposition "whose actual truth value is its only possible truth value." Hence, an *a priori* true proposition is a necessarily true proposition.) Now since the proposition "There exists a logically necessary being" is, if true, necessarily true, it follows, if Kennick is correct, both that no premises can provide *evidence* for that proposition and that that proposition cannot be a *deductive consequence* of any true proposition or conjunction of true propositions. But if an argument is a proof of its conclusion, then its conclusion must be a deductive consequence of its true premises, and its premises must provide evidence for its conclusion.

Why does Kennick believe that if q is necessarily true it cannot be a deductive consequence of any proposition or conjunction of propositions? The crucial step in his reasoning to this end is the following: "For q is a deductive consequence of p if and only if 'p and not-q' is necessarily false and the necessary falsity of 'p and not-q' can be removed by the removal of p."[14] Since by hypothesis q (i.e., "There exists a necessary being") is necessarily true, it is clear that the necessary falsity of

[13] See "On Proving That God Exists" in Sidney Hook, ed., *Religious Experience and Truth* (New York: New York University Press, 1961), pp. 261-269.

[14] *Ibid.*, pp. 265-266.

"p and not-q" is not removed by the removal of p. For not-q will itself be necessarily false. Hence, it follows from Kennick's stipulation of conditions for the relation of deductive consequence that no necessarily true proposition can be a deductive consequence of any other propositions. But surely

1. 9 is greater than 7.

is a deductive consequence of the conjunction of

2. The number of planets is 9.

and

3. The number of planets is greater than 7.

On Kennick's view, however, (1) cannot be a deductive consequence of any proposition or conjunction of propositions for it is an *a priori* truth. Thus his view implies that the conclusion of a rigorous mathematical proof is not a deductive consequence of the premises in its proof. I take the absurdity of this result to be sufficient justification for rejecting Kennick's claim that q is a deductive consequence of p only if the necessary falsity of "p and not-q" can be removed by the removal of p.

Kennick's second reason is that if q is *a priori* true then p cannot be *evidence* for q. His argument is as follows:

> For whatever empirical proposition, true or false, is substituted for p or is made a conjunct of p, p implies q if q is *a priori* true. To put the point in another way: everything and anything is evidence for the existence of God, which means that nothing is evidence for the existence of God.[15]

[15] *Ibid.*, p. 265.

Clearly if Kennick's argument is correct, the following principle must be accepted:

> *A. If a certain proposition implies q, then that proposition is evidence for q only if every proposition that implies q is evidence for q.*

Given (A) and

> *B. Every proposition implies an* a priori *true proposition.*

it follows that if the conclusion of the Cosmological Argument is *a priori* true then either its premises do not constitute evidence for it or every proposition is evidence for it. Since, as Kennick supposes, it would be absurd to take every proposition (whether true or false) as evidence for the conclusion of the Cosmological Argument, it follows—given its status as a necessary truth—that the premises of the Cosmological Argument do not provide evidence for its conclusion.

Kennick's argument rests on (A) or some principle that entails (A). But (A) is not true. Clearly

> *1. John is a bachelor.*

and

> *2. If any man is a bachelor, he is unmarried.*

imply

> *3. John is unmarried.*

Moreover, we may regard the conjunction of (1) and (2) as *evidence* for the truth of (3). However, given (A), it then would follow that since

> *4. It is raining.*

and

The Idea of a Necessary Being

5. *It is not raining.*

imply (3), the conjunction of (4) and (5) is *evidence* for the truth of (3). Again,

6. *(3 × 3) is 9.*

and

7. *9 is greater than 7.*

imply

8. *(3 × 3) is greater than 7.*

We may regard (6) and (7) as conclusive *evidence* for (8). But since (8) is *a priori* true,

9. *Snow is not white.*

also implies (8). And given (A) it follows that (9) is evidence for the truth of (8). This example, as well as the previous one, shows that (A) is false. Since Kennick's second reason why the conclusion of the Cosmological Argument—if the argument is to be a proof of its conclusion—cannot be necessarily true rests on a false principle, we may safely reject it.

We must now consider the more serious objection to the Cosmological Argument, the objection that it is impossible for there to be a necessary being in the sense of a logically necessary being. In some respects this is the most formidable objection to the Cosmological Argument. For other objections endeavor to show that some premise in the argument is not known to be true or is inferred from propositions that do not entail it or are not themselves known to be true. That is, several objections, if correct, show only that the soundness of the Cosmological Argument has not been *established*;

they do not show that the argument is unsound. The present objection, however, purports to establish that there can be no being whose existence is logically necessary. If this objection is correct, the conclusion of the Cosmological Argument is false—and what better grounds could we have for rejecting an argument than the sure knowledge that its conclusion is false? Indeed, even if some other objection purports to show that one of the premises of the Cosmological Argument is false, it would not be so formidable as the present objection. For we might find other premises of a suitable sort to serve in place of the rejected premise. But since the whole purpose of the Cosmological Argument is to establish the existence of a necessary being, if it is shown that there cannot be such a being, then the Cosmological Argument, no matter what premises it employs, is doomed to fail.

That it is impossible for there to be a logically necessary being, a being whose non-existence is a logical impossibility, is taken by many critics of theism to be a fundamental feature of philosophy since Hume and Kant.[16] Indeed, some defenders of theism hold the view that it has been conclusively established that the idea of a logically necessary being is a self-contradictory idea. Thus John Hick remarks: "There cannot—logically cannot—be a being whose non-existence is logically impossible. I conclude then that we must on philosophical grounds repudiate all talk of God as having necessary being, where the necessity in question is construed as

[16] See, for example, J. N. Findlay, "Can God's Existence Be Disproved?" *Mind*, Vol. 57 (1948); J.J.C. Smart, "The Existence of God"; and Paul Edwards, "The Cosmological Argument," *The Rationalist Annual* for 1959.

logical necessity."[17] What, then, are these philosophical grounds central to modern philosophy that supposedly *demonstrate* that there cannot be a being whose existence is logically necessary?

One point frequently made against the idea of a necessary being is that, as J.J.C. Smart expresses it, ". . . 'necessary' is a predicate of *propositions*, not of things."[18] The point of this objection—it is somewhat overstated—is not that it makes no sense to speak of a necessary being; rather, the point is that "necessary" belongs *primarily* to propositions and can be applied to beings only if the application is explained in reference to some proposition being necessary. Thus Smart goes on to remark: "Now since 'necessary' is a word which applies primarily to propositions, we shall have to interpret 'God is a necessary being' as 'The proposition "God exists" is logically necessary.' "[19] Smart's view, apparently, is that the result of substituting a singular term for x in "x is a necessary being" will yield a true proposition only if the result of putting the *same* singular term for x in "x exists" will yield a logically necessary proposition. Expressed in this way, the requirement seems too strong. For anyone who holds that God is a necessary being and believes that the object of Eckhart's contemplation is identical with God also would hold that the object of Eckhart's contemplation is a necessary being. But while he might be prepared to view "God exists" as a necessary truth, he would not be prepared to view "The object of Eckhart's contemplation exists"

[17] John Hick, "Necessary Being," *Scottish Journal of Theology* (December 1961), p. 356.
[18] "The Existence of God," p. 38.
[19] *Ibid.*

as a necessary truth. Perhaps then we might weaken the requirement as follows: x is a logically necessary being only if *some proposition* affirming the existence of the being that is x is logically necessary. On this weaker requirement, it could be true that the result of substituting a singular term for x in "x is a necessary being" will yield a true proposition even though the result of putting the same singular term for x in "x exists" will not yield a logically necessary proposition. Presumably this weaker requirement would satisfy Smart, since it does tie the idea of a necessary being to the idea of some affirmative existential proposition's being logically necessary.

I am inclined to accept this first point about the idea of a logically necessary being. What could we mean in saying that there exists a being whose existence is logically necessary if we also claimed that no proposition that asserts the existence of a thing is logically necessary? We can, of course, assert that there exists a necessary being in the sense of a factually or causally necessary being and also claim that all affirmative, existential propositions are contingent. But what is at stake here is the conclusion of the eighteenth-century form of the Cosmological Argument. And as we have seen, the conclusion of that argument asserts that there exists a *logically* necessary being. And the question here is whether we could consistently affirm the existence of such a being while denying that any affirmative, existential statements are logically necessary. It seems to me that we cannot. Consequently, I think it is fair to concede this first point to the critics of the idea of a logically necessary being.

The central objections to the idea of a logically necessary being presuppose the point just discussed; they presuppose, that is, that x is a logically necessary being only if some proposition asserting the existence of x is logically necessary. Since we have granted this point, we can now turn to an examination of the two central objections that seem to be a part of modern empiricist philosophy. Each of these objections endeavors to establish that no proposition that asserts the real existence of something can be logically necessary. If the objections succeed, then, granted the first point, it will follow that there cannot be a necessary being in the sense of a logically necessary being, and, hence, that the conclusion of the Cosmological Argument is false.

The first of the two objections derives its force from two fundamental claims. The first claim is that a necessary proposition is one in which *concepts* are related in certain ways, i.e., by way of inclusion as in "Whatever is a bachelor is unmarried" (the concept "unmarried" is included in the concept "bachelor") or by way of exclusion as in "No triangle is a four-sided figure" (the concept "triangle" excludes the concept "four-sided figure"). The second claim is that an affirmative existential proposition is not a proposition in which concepts are related. This point is sometimes put by saying that an affirmative, existential proposition does not say that one concept is related in a certain way to another concept, but that a concept applies to something. Thus J.J.C. Smart remarks: "No existential proposition can be logically necessary, for we saw that the truth of a logically necessary proposition depends . . . on the relationship of concepts. We saw, however, . . . that an existential proposition does not say that one concept is involved in another, but that a concept applies to something."[20] Another way in which the second fundamental claim is

[20] *Ibid.*, pp. 38-39.

sometimes put is by saying that existence is not a characteristic or real predicate and, therefore, cannot be contained in a concept, as it would have to be if an existential statement were logically necessary. Thus after claiming that if an existential proposition were necessary, existence (in at least one case) would be contained in a concept, Paul Edwards remarks: "But only a characteristic can be contained in a concept and it has seemed plain to most philosophers since Kant that existence is not a characteristic, that it can hence never be contained in a concept, and that hence no existential statement can ever be a necessary truth."[21]

Smart and Edwards provide us with two versions of the first objection to the idea of a logically necessary being. Smart's version of the objection proceeds as follows:

1. A logically necessary proposition says truly that one concept is involved in another.

2. An existential proposition does not say that one concept is involved in another, but that a concept applies to something.

Therefore:

3. No existential proposition is logically necessary.

And Edwards's version of the objection can be expressed in terms of the following argument:

1. If an existential proposition is logically necessary then in at least one case existence is contained in a concept.

[21] Paul Edwards, "The Cosmological Argument," reprinted in Donald R. Burrill, ed., *The Cosmological Arguments*, p. 116.

2. *Only a characteristic can be contained in a concept, and existence is not a characteristic.*

Therefore:

3. *No existential proposition is logically necessary.*

I propose to examine these two versions as representative of the first of the two major objections to the idea of a logically necessary being.

The second premises of the above arguments present two related, basic ideas in modern empiricist philosophy. These ideas are (i) that existence is not a characteristic that things may or may not have, and (ii) that when we assert, for example, that God exists we are not ascribing a characteristic to some object but are saying that the concept "God" is exemplified, applies to something. Although these two ideas may be mistaken, I think we can defend the idea of a logically necessary being without having to deny either (i) or (ii). Moreover, it is perhaps worth noting that the question of whether or not there is or can be a logically necessary being is independent of the question of whether existence is a characteristic that may be included in the definition of a concept. For as I argued earlier, what follows from including existence in a concept is not that there exists something that satisfies that concept but only that no non-existing thing can satisfy that concept. Similarly, the result of including necessary existence in a concept is not that some necessarily existing thing satisfies that concept but only that no non-existing or contingently existing thing satisfies that concept.

Suppose that we concede that an affirmative existential proposition such as "God exists" is to be understood as asserting that the concept "God" is exemplified, applies to something. Why then cannot the proposition "God exists" be logically necessary? The answer is that, so understood, the proposition "God exists" does not assert that one concept is involved in another and, as the first premise of Smart's argument assures us, for a proposition to be logically necessary it must assert truly that one concept is involved in another concept.

The weakness of the first major objection to the idea of a logically necessary being lies, it seems to me, in its criterion for logical necessity, in its fundamental claim that a proposition is necessary *only if* it asserts that concepts are related in a certain manner.[22] There are, of course, logically necessary propositions that are necessary for reasons other than the inclusion or exclusion of concepts—e.g., propositions of the form "p or not-p." But in fairness to the proponents of the first objection we should perhaps construe the first premise as a claim not about any logically necessary proposition whatever but about any logically necessary proposition expressed by a sentence that grammatically is a subject-predicate sentence. Since an affirmative existential statement, whether general (e.g., "Lions exist") or singular (e.g., "God exists"), is grammatically of the subject-predicate form, it is sufficient to claim only that logically necessary statements of the subject-predicate grammatical form are logically necessary by virtue of the inclusion or exclusion of one concept in (from) another. Thus, in an affirmative subject-predicate statement, e.g., "Every

[22] For an incisive and illuminating discussion of this and related points see Robert Merrihew Adams, "Has It Been Proved That All Real Existence Is Contingent," *American Philosophical Quarterly*, Vol. 8, No. 3 (July 1971), pp. 284-291.

bachelor is unmarried," we have an instance of a necessary truth in which one concept "unmarried" is included in another concept "bachelor"; and in a negative, subject-predicate statement, e.g., "No triangle is a four-sided figure," we have an instance of a necessary truth in which one concept, "four-sided figure," is excluded from another concept "triangle."

My objection to the claim that any necessary statement (grammatically of the subject-predicate form) is necessary by virtue of the inclusion or exclusion of the concepts occurring in it is not that the claim is false but that no one has established that it is true. Of course, if the claim is true then, given that an affirmative existential statement does not assert that one concept is included in another, it will follow that no affirmative existential statement can be necessary. So, granted our earlier discussion, if there is a being whose existence is logically necessary, the claim now under investigation is false. But in order to respond to the first major objection to the idea of a logically necessary being we need not show that the claim in question is false, only that it has not been established as true. And I think it is fair to say that no one has established that the claim in question is true. At best, it seems to me, the proponent of the first objection can argue that the only way in which he can *see* how an affirmative subject-predicate statement could be necessary is by the predicate-concept being included in the subject-concept or by some such relation of concepts. But this, of course, does not constitute a *proof* of the claim in question. It is, after all, one thing for a proposition to be necessarily true and quite another thing to *see* that and how it is necessarily true. Of course, if we can see that and how certain statements are necessary and cannot see that and how other statements (e.g., affirmative, existential statements) could be necessary, that may give us some reason for thinking that they are not necessary. But it hardly gives us a proof. Nor does it give us adequate grounds for rejecting *in advance* any argument that might be put forth to show that at least one affirmative, existential statement is necessarily true. The Cosmological Argument and various forms of the Ontological Argument purport to establish that there exists a being whose existence is logically necessary, that there is at least one affirmative existential statement that is necessarily true. If we have a proof that no affirmative, existential statement can be logically necessary, then we have a proof that the Cosmological Argument and these versions of the Ontological Argument are unsound. But we do not have a proof. At best we have some reason for thinking that affirmative, existential statements are all contingent. And this reason must be weighed against whatever rational grounds the Cosmological Argument and some versions of the Ontological Argument provide us for thinking that at least one affirmative, existential statement is necessary. The first objection, then, does not establish that the conclusion of the Cosmological Argument is false and, therefore, does not establish that the argument is unsound.

The second major objection to the idea of a logically necessary being rests, like the first, on the point that there is a logically necessary being only if some affirmative, existential statement is logically necessary. The objection itself derives its force from a modern view of necessity sometimes called "conventionalism." According to this view, "necessity in propositions merely reflects our use of words, the arbitrary conventions of our language."[23] A statement is necessary not because it records some necessary fact about reality but because of the way in which we use words; if we used our symbols differently, the statement in question would not be necessary. Necessary propositions, according to the conventionalist's view, provide no information about the non-linguistic world, they merely enlighten us by illustrating the way we use certain symbols. As Ayer once remarked:

> Thus if I say, "Nothing can be coloured in different ways at the same time with respect to the same part of itself," I am not saying anything about the properties of any actual thing; but I am not talking nonsense. I am expressing an analytic proposition, which records *our determination* to call a colour expanse which differs in quality from a neighboring colour expanse a different part of a given thing. In other words, I am simply calling attention to the implications of a certain linguistic usage.[24]

Conventionalism, as I have described it, provides, I think, two distinct reasons for rejecting the idea of a logically necessary being. First, as we have seen, according to the conventionalist's view, a proposition is necessarily true solely because of our rules for the use of the symbols contained in the proposition. But surely the truth of an affirmative, existential statement depends on what reality contains and not simply on our decisions concerning the use of linguistic symbols. Second, on the conventionalist's view, necessarily true propositions provide us with no information about the non-linguistic world, they merely provide us with information about

[23] J. N. Findlay, "Can God's Existence Be Disproved?" p. 54.
[24] A. J. Ayer, *Language, Truth and Logic* (New York: Dover Publications), p. 79. Italics mine.

our use of symbols. But surely an affirmative, existential statement, if true, provides us with some information concerning the constituents of the real world. It cannot be that an affirmative, existential statement, if true, tells us nothing about the real world. Therefore, no affirmative, existential statement can be necessarily true.

The weakness of the second major objection to the idea of a logically necessary being is its reliance on the conventionalist's theory of necessary truth. Part of what the objection says about affirmative, existential statements seems correct—their truth depends on what reality contains and not simply on our determination to use symbols in certain ways. But the conventionalist's claims about necessity are open to serious objection. Of course, whether a given indicative sentence expresses a truth will depend *in part* on the meaning of the words in the sentence. This is so of sentences expressing contingent truths as well as of sentences expressing necessary truths. If we used "lions" to mean what we mean by "tigers," the sentence "There are lions in Africa" would express a falsehood rather than a truth. But that a necessary truth should be true *solely* by virtue of the way in which we use words and, therefore, independently of the nature of reality seems unlikely. For given the way we use words, it still appears to be a necessary condition for the truth of "No triangle is a four-sided figure" that the property of being a triangle *excludes* the property of being four-sided—and this last seems to be a matter of how properties are related and not of the ways in which we use words. Thus the conventionalist's view that necessity merely reflects our use of words, the arbitrary conventions of our language, seems false. But in defending the Cosmological Argument against this objection it is not essential to hold that conventionalism is false, only that it has not been established. So long as conventionalism is not established, the second objection, while it may raise some doubts about the idea of a logically necessary being, is not a *proof* that there is no such being. Consequently whatever force the objection has, it cannot show that the Cosmological Argument is unsound. At best, it, like the first objection, provides us with some reasons, perhaps, for thinking that the conclusion of the Cosmological Argument is false. These reasons must be weighed in the balance with whatever rational grounds the Cosmological Argument provides us for thinking that its conclusion is true.

V

Must a Self-Existent, Necessary Being Be God?

AT the outset of this study, we noted that as an argument for the existence of the theistic God the Cosmological Argument must be understood as having two parts. In the eighteenth-century version set forth by Samuel Clarke, the first part consists of an argument to establish the existence of a necessary being. The second part of the argument consists of a series of arguments by which Clarke endeavors to establish that the necessary being has the properties definitive of the theistic idea of God. Having completed our study of the first part of the argument, we can now turn our attention to its second part. We shall not, however, consider every property that Clarke endeavors to prove must belong to the necessary being, nor shall we consider every argument he gives for the possession by the necessary being of those properties we do consider. Instead, we shall select several of the more important properties associated with the theistic concept of God and consider only what appear to be the strongest of Clarke's arguments to prove their possession by the necessary being. Specifically, we shall consider the major arguments by which Clarke proposes to establish that the being whose existence he has established in the first part of the Cosmological Argument is *eternal, infinite* (omnipresent), *omniscient, omnipotent,* and *infinitely good.* It is fair to say that these properties are definitive of the theistic

222

concept of God. Hence, Clarke's Cosmological Argument is an argument to establish the existence of the theistic God.

Before we consider the second part of the Cosmological Argument, it will be helpful to remind ourselves of what the first part of the Cosmological Argument purports to establish. I have characterized the conclusion of the first part as "There exists a necessary being." But in the course of establishing the existence of a necessary being, Clarke actually shows that this necessary being has two further features, features he draws upon in developing the second part of the Cosmological Argument. The first part of the Cosmological Argument purports to establish that there exists a being

   i. *that is a necessary being—its existence is logically necessary,*

   ii. *that is self-existent—has the explanation of its existence within its own nature,*

and,

   iii. *that accounts for the fact that there are dependent beings.*

With these features in mind, we can now examine the arguments by which Clarke hopes to establish that the being that has these features must also have the properties definitive of the theistic idea of God.

Having argued that there exists a being that accounts for the fact that there is a world, which is self-existent, and which cannot not exist, Clarke begins the development of the second part of the Cosmological Argument by contending that the being in question must be *eternal.* By "eternal," theologians have meant either of two quite distinct things. The major theologians of the medieval period held that God is eternal in the sense of being *timeless.* To be eternal, on their view, is not to have infinite duration in both temporal directions, but to exist outside of time altogether. Thus Anselm remarks:

> Thou wast not, then, yesterday, nor wilt thou be to-morrow; but yesterday and today and tomorrow thou art; or, rather, neither yesterday nor today nor tomor-row thou art; but simply, thou art, outside all time. For yesterday and today and tomorrow have no exist-ence, except in time; but thou, although nothing exists without thee, nevertheless dost not exist in space or time, but all things exist in thee. For nothing contains thee, but thou containest all.[1]

The second meaning of "eternal" is *everlasting.* To be eternal in this sense is to exist in time and to have neither beginning nor end. It is in this latter sense that Clarke understands that God is eternal. He was not un-aware of the medieval view. He simply rejected it as an unintelligible notion.

Clarke's major argument to establish that the self-existent, necessary being is eternal runs as follows:

> To be self-existent is (as has been already shown) to exist by an absolute necessity in the nature of the thing itself. Now this necessity being absolute, and not de-pending upon anything external, must be always un-alterably the same; nothing being alterable, but what is capable of being affected by somewhat without itself. That being therefore, which has no other cause of its existence but the absolute necessity of its own nature, must of necessity have existed from everlasting, without

[1] *Proslogion,* Chapter XIX.

beginning, and must of necessity exist to everlasting without end (*Demonstration*, pp. 41-42).

Clarke's argument here is somewhat unclear. Perhaps the most likely interpretation is the following:

1. *What is changeable is capable of being changed by something external to itself.*
2. *A self-existent being cannot be changed by something external to itself.*

Therefore:

3. *A self-existent being is not changeable.*

Therefore:

4. *A self-existent being must be always unalterably the same.*

Therefore:

5. *A self-existent being if it exists at all must always have existed and must exist to everlasting without end.*

On this interpretation, Clarke's argument rests simply on the idea of self-existence. He endeavors to show that a self-existent being is unchangeable and, therefore, must be eternal. For if it were to have come into existence or to cease existing it would not be unchangeable.

Another possible interpretation of Clarke's argument is to view it as resting not solely on the idea of self-existence, but on both the notion of self-existence and the fundamental principle that if something comes into existence or ceases to exist it is dependent for its existence on something outside itself. On this interpretation we have:

1. *A self-existent being does not depend for its existence on any other being.*

2. *If something comes into existence then it depends for its existence on that being that produced it.*

Therefore:

3. *A self-existent being cannot have come into existence.*

4. *If something ceases to exist then it depends for its existence on something outside itself.*

Therefore:

5. *A self-existent being cannot cease to exist.*

Therefore:

6. *A self-existent being, if it exists, must have eternal existence.*

Either of these arguments may be sufficient to show that a self-existent, necessary being must be eternal. But, as I have indicated, the passage cited from Clarke does not clearly indicate which of these arguments he is advancing. In any case, it seems reasonably clear that Clarke is right in his contention that a self-existent, necessary being must be an eternal being. For if a being came into existence at a certain time, then either it was produced by some other being or its coming into existence was simply a brute fact. In either case, however, the being in question would *not* be one whose existence is entirely and solely accounted for by reference to its own nature. So, clearly, a self-existent being, if it exists, must have existed from everlasting, without beginning. It is somewhat more difficult to see why a self-existent being cannot perish. For while a thing cannot bring itself into existence it seems that we might sometimes account for the perishing of a thing in terms of that thing itself. Why, then, cannot a self-existent being perish? If something perishes, then either something else caused it to perish, it caused itself to perish, or its perishing is a brute fact. In the first case, the object in question would be dependent for its existence on the non-operation of that force by which the other thing caused it to perish, and, hence, would not be a self-existent being. In the last two cases, we must suppose a change in the nature of the thing in question. For its very nature is sufficient to account for its existence. But the nature of a thing is precisely what cannot undergo change. Therefore, it seems that a self-existent, necessary being must be an eternal being, a being that exists from everlasting to everlasting.

Clarke offers both a direct and a reductio argument to show that a self-existent being must be *infinite*. The direct "proof" is as follows:

> To be self-existent . . . is to exist by an absolute necessity in the nature of the thing itself. Now this necessity being absolute in itself, and not depending on any outward cause, it is evident it must be every *where*, as well as *always*, unalterably the same. For a necessity which is not everywhere the same, is plainly a consequential necessity only, depending upon some external cause, and not an absolute one in its own nature. For a necessity absolutely such in itself has no relation to time and place, or anything else. Whatever therefore exists by an absolute necessity in its own nature must needs be infinite as well as eternal (*Demonstration*, p. 44).

Apparently Clarke thinks there is a parallel to be drawn between spatial infinity and temporal infinity. Just as a self-existent being must exist at every moment of time, so too it must exist at every point in space. Otherwise its necessity would bear a dependence on some other being which determined it to exist at just those moments of time or at just those points in space.

In presenting a reductio argument Clarke claims that it is logically impossible for any finite being to be a self-existent being. Clearly if he is right about this then a self-existent being must be infinite, since any existing being is either finite or infinite.

> To suppose a finite being to be self-existent is to say that it is a contradiction for that being not to exist, the absence of which may yet be conceived without a contradiction. Which is the greatest absurdity in the world. For if a being can without a contradiction be absent from one place, it may without a contradiction be absent likewise from another place, and from all places. And whatever necessity it may have of existing must arise from some external cause, and not absolutely from itself. And consequently, the being cannot be self-existent (*Demonstration*, pp. 45-46).

The principle on which this argument turns may be expressed as:

A. *If it is possible for x to be absent from one place then it is possible for x to be absent from every place.*

Given (A) and the principle that if something exists it must exist in some place, it certainly follows that no finite being can be a self-existent being. For to be finite a being must lack existence at some place, otherwise it would have existence at every place and, therefore, be infinite. Since a finite being lacks existence at some place, the antecedent of (A) will be true of it.

Hence, given (A), the finite being in question will not be a necessary being.

Is (A) true? In an interesting exchange of letters, Joseph Butler, then a college student, challenged Clarke on precisely this question. In order to understand Butler's challenge, we need to refine (A) by introducing temporal issues. Consider the following two principles:

> i. *If it is possible for x to be absent from one place at a certain time then for any place you pick there is a time at which it is possible that x does not exist at that place.*

and,

> ii. *If it is possible for x to be absent from one place at a certain time then there is a certain time such that for any place you pick it is possible for x to be absent from that place at that time.*

The consequent of (ii) affirms that there is a certain time such that it is possible that x exists *nowhere* at that time. The consequent of (i), however, affirms only that for each place there is some time or other when it is possible that x does not exist at that place. The consequent of (ii) formally implies the consequent of (i), but is not formally implied by the consequent of (i). In asserting (A), Clarke intends to be asserting (ii). He thinks that if it is possible for something to be absent from a certain place at time t then it follows that it is possible for that thing to be absent from every place at that time t. Butler, however, thinks that all that follows is that it is possible for that thing to be absent from every place at different times. Thus in his first letter to Clarke he remarks:

> . . . all that it proves is that if a being can, without contradiction, be absent from one place at one time, it may without a contradiction be absent from another place, and so from all places, at different times; (for I cannot see that if a being can be absent from *one place* at *one time*, therefore, it may without contradiction be absent from *all places* at the *same time*, i.e., may cease to exist.)²

Perhaps we can put Butler's point as follows. Either (A) expresses (i) or it expresses (ii). If it expresses (i) then (A) is true but the argument will not show that a finite being cannot be self-existent. If (A) expresses (ii) then (A) is false. In either case Clarke's argument fails to establish that a self-existent being cannot be finite.

Responding to Butler, Clarke makes it clear that he intends (A) to express (ii). Indeed, in beginning his response Clarke asserts something stronger than (ii); namely,

> iii. *If it is possible for x to be absent from one place at a certain time then it is possible for x to be absent from all places at all times.*

Thus he remarks:

> Whatever may, without a contradiction, be absent from any one place at any one time may also, without a contradiction, be absent from all places at all times. For whatever is necessary at all is absolutely necessary in

² This letter and the further correspondence between Butler and Clarke are published with the later editions of Clarke's *Demonstration*. For the passage quoted see *Demonstration*, pp. 460-461.

every part of space, and in every point of duration. Whatever can at any time be conceived possible to be absent from any one part of space, may for the same reason (viz., the implying no contradiction in the nature of things) be conceived possible to be absent from every other part of space at the same time, either by ceasing to be or by supposing it never to have begun to be.[3]

Of course, as a response to Butler's objection, what Clarke here says begs the very question at issue. For Butler is saying that although he accepts the truth of (i), he cannot see why he should accept either (ii) or (iii). In his response Clarke simply asserts (ii) and (iii) without giving any reasons for accepting them.

It is not until his response to Butler's third letter that Clarke satisfies Butler on the question of the truth of (A)—where (A) is taken to express (ii). The key passage in the letter is the following:

Determination of a particular quantity, or particular time or place of existence of any thing, cannot arise but from somewhat *external* to the thing itself. For example: why there should exist just such a small determinate quantity of matter, neither more nor less, interspersed in the immense vacuities of space, no reason can be given. To suppose matter, or any other substance, necessarily-existing in a finite determinate quantity; in an inch-cube, for instance or in any certain number of cube-inches, and no more, is exactly the same absurdity as supposing it to exist necessarily, and yet for a finite duration only, which everyone sees to be a plain contradiction.[4]

---

[3] *Ibid.*, pp. 464-465.   [4] *Ibid.*, pp. 475-476.

Apparently these remarks by Clarke persuaded Butler to accept (ii), for in his next letter Butler writes: ". . . it now seems to me altogether unreasonable to suppose absolute necessity can have any relation to one part of space more than to another; and, if so, an absolutely-necessary being must exist *everywhere*."[5] Presumably, the point that persuaded Butler is Clarke's contention that if x exists only in a certain part of space something *external* to x must have brought it about that x exists in just that part of space rather than in some other part. As we noted, a point like this is stressed in Clarke's direct argument for the infinity of a self-existent being. This point about space may draw some force from the parallel point about time: namely, if x exists only in a part of time something *external* to x must have brought it about that x exists in just that part of time rather than in some other part.

In the light of Clarke's exchange with Butler, we can perhaps put Clarke's fundamental argument for the infinity of a self-existent being as follows:

1. If x is finite than x exists only in a certain part of space.

2. If x exists only in a certain part of space, then something external to x brought it about that x exists in a certain part of space rather than some other part.

3. If something external to x brought it about that x exists in a certain part of space rather than another part then x is not a self-existent, necessary being.

Therefore:

5 *Ibid.*, p. 478.

4. *No finite being is a self-existent, necessary being.*

Therefore:

5. *A self-existent, necessary being is an infinite being.*

Like Butler, I find myself persuaded by this argument. One underlying assumption, however, which might be questioned is Clarke's conviction that beings are all in space and time, that the notion of a spaceless or timeless being is unintelligible. Just as Anselm held that God is outside time, so he held that God is outside space. But given Clarke's assumption that if a being exists it exists somewhere or everywhere, his argument, I think, provides us with some good reasons for thinking that a self-existent, necessary being must be infinite.

In discussing infinity, Clarke distinguishes between an infinity of *immensity* and an infinity of *fullness*, pointing out that a self-existent being must have an infinity both of immensity and fullness. To have an infinity of immensity is to be boundless, without limits. Something like matter, say, could be boundless even though it has some empty spots, "vacuities," and, therefore, lacks an infinity of fullness. The same basic argument by which Clarke endeavored to prove the infinity of a self-existent being can be adapted to show that a self-existent being has both an infinity of immensity and an infinity of fullness.

Thus far Clarke has tried to show the infinity of the self-existent being. But infinity is not quite the same idea as *omnipresence*. If we mean by "x is omnipresent" simply that x itself or *some part of x* is present at every point in the boundless immensity of space, then to be omnipresent would be equivalent to having an infinity of immensity and an infinity of fullness. Matter, for example, if it were spread out fully in the immensity of boundless space would be omnipresent in this sense. But what Clarke intends to convey by the idea of omnipresence—at least, as that idea is applied to a self-existent being—is that of being *fully present* at each point of the boundless immensity. Thus he remarks:

> The supreme cause on the contrary, being an infinite and most simple essence, and comprehending all things perfectly in himself, is *at all times equally* present, both in his simple essence, and by the immediate and perfect exercise of all his attributes, to every point of the boundless immensity, as if it were really all but one single point (*Demonstration*, p. 47).

We are not to think that a self-existent being is not a single being but has somehow multiplied itself so that it can be wholly present at each point in space. For this would destroy the unity of the self-existent being. But short of picturing the self-existent being as infinitely multiplied it is difficult to form any coherent picture of how such a being could be *wholly present* at every point in space at every moment of time. Clarke seems to admit as much:

> But as to the *particular manner* of his being infinite or everywhere present, in opposition to the manner of created things being present in such or such finite places; this is as impossible for our finite understandings to comprehend or explain, as it is for us to form an adequate idea of infinity (*Demonstration*, p. 46).

It is clear from the above that no physical thing could be omnipresent in the sense in which Clarke thinks the self-existent being is omnipresent. For any physical object, even if we imagine it to have immensity, cannot be *wholly present* at each point in space. One spatial part may be wholly present at one part of space and another spatial part of that object may be wholly present at another part of space. But the object itself cannot be *wholly present* at each of those parts of space.

But why should we think that a self-existent being is omnipresent in Clarke's sense? Indeed, why should we think that a self-existent being is not some sort of infinite physical body or bare matter? In answer to these questions, Clarke relies on two sorts of arguments. For those who propose that matter is the infinite substance, Clarke appeals to certain empirical experiments that he thinks show that matter lacks an infinity of fullness. Since a self-existent being has an infinity both of immensity and fullness, the experiments provide grounds for rejecting the view that matter is a self-existent substance. The experiments in question had to do with the unequal resistance of different fluids to pressure. Clarke thought that if all space were filled with matter the resistance of all fluids should be equal.

The second, and philosophically more interesting sort of argument is designed to show that a self-existent being must be "a most simple, unchangeable, incorruptible being; without parts, figure, motion, divisibility." If Clarke can show this, then, since whatever is physical is extended in space and can be divided into *spatial parts*, it will follow that a self-existent being is not a physical substance. Moreover, if it is shown that a self-existent being has no parts whatever, then since it is infinite, it must be *wholly present* at each point in space; otherwise only a part of it would be present at a certain point in space and, consequently, it would be divisible into spatial parts. Clearly these are issues of fundamental importance to the second part of the Cosmological Argument. Unfortunately, Clarke's remarks on these issues are so brief that it is difficult to determine their worth and not even clear what they mean. It is clear that he thinks the concepts of "parts," "figure," "motion," and "divisibility" all imply *finiteness*. "For all these things do plainly and necessarily imply finiteness in their very notion, and are utterly inconsistent with complete infinity" (*Demonstration*, p. 45). What is less than clear is that these concepts do imply finiteness. An infinitely extended body, it seems, might be divisible into an infinite number of spatial parts. If so, the mere idea of having parts does not appear to imply finiteness. Hence, although Clarke's reasoning to show that a self-existent being must have both an infinity of immensity and an infinity of fullness is rather cogent, his proof that a self-existent being must be omnipresent in the sense of being *wholly present* at each point in the boundless immensity of space rests on the unsupported and rather questionable claim that anything that has parts or is in any way divisible must of necessity be finite.

That a self-existent being must be an *intelligent* being is, Clarke admits, much more difficult to prove than that a self-existent being must be eternal and infinite. The reason for this, Clarke suggests, is that we cannot "see the immediate and necessary connection of it with self-existence, as we can that of eternity, infinity, unity, etc." (*Demonstration*, p. 51). How, then, is it to be shown that the self-existent being is intelligent? If we wish to show that a self-existent being has a certain feature F we can either reason *a priori*, trying to demonstrate a necessary connection between self-existence and F, or we can proceed *a posteriori*, reasoning that the presence of F in our world can be accounted for only (or best) by supposing that the self-existent being caused F to exist in the world and must, therefore, itself possess F. Clarke's view is that, unlike eternity and infinity, intelligence is a feature whose possession by a self-existent being cannot be shown by *a priori* reasoning—not because there is no necessary connection between self-existence and intelligence but because our limited minds are unable to perceive it. His procedure is to use the *a posteriori* method in reasoning that the self-existent being is intelligent.

We can represent the structure of Clarke's argument as follows:

1. *Intelligence is a perfection.*
2. *Intelligence exists in the world, particularly in man.*
3. *Whatever perfection exists in the world must also exist in the original cause of the world—otherwise something comes from nothing.*
4. *The self-existent being is the original cause of the world.*

Therefore:

5. *The self-existent being must be intelligent.*

In critically assessing this argument, we must keep in mind that in the first part of the Cosmological Argument it was argued not only that there is a necessary, self-existent being but that this being accounts for the fact that there is a world of dependent things. Second, when Clarke speaks of "The self-existent being," as in premise (4), we must not suppose that he is naively assuming that there can be only one such being. Although his reasoning may be faulty, Clarke has used the *a priori* method to show that there can be only one self-existent being. Consequently, by the time he turns to consider the feature of intelligence, he feels entitled to speak of the (one and only) self-existent being.

Granting premise (4) of Clarke's argument, what are we to say about (3)? A premise like (3) was accepted by the major medieval theologians and also asserted by Descartes. Clarke advances this premise in the following passage:

> . . . the self-existent being, whatever that be supposed to be, must of necessity (being the original of all things) contain in itself the sum and highest degree of all the perfections of all things. Not because that which is self-existent must therefore have all possible perfections (for this, though most certainly true in itself, yet cannot be so easily demonstrated *a priori*). But because it is impossible that any effect should have any perfection which was not in the cause. For if it had, then that perfection would be caused by nothing; which is a plain contradiction. Now an *unintelligent* being, it is evident, cannot be endued with all the perfections of all things in the world; because intelligence is one of those perfections. All things therefore cannot arise from an unintelligent original. And consequently the self-existing being, must of necessity be intelligent (*Demonstration*, pp. 51-52).

Clarke considers two sorts of objections to premise (3). First, it might be objected that the objects in the physical world possess only primary qualities (figure, divisibility, motion, etc.) and yet are able to cause the secondary qualities of color, taste, sound, etc. Therefore, it cannot be true that the cause must have all the positive qualities contained in its effects. Second, the qualities of matter—motion, divisibility, figure, etc.— must have God as their original cause. But no one, including Clarke, can believe that God himself has these qualities. Consequently, it is not true that the cause must itself have all the perfections and positive properties contained in its effects.

To the first objection, Clarke denies that the material objects in the world actually cause colors, sounds, and tastes. They at best occasion the experience of colors, etc., by acting on something (the mind) that Clarke holds to be not a material substance, but a conscious, perceiving, experiencing substance. The real cause, then, on Clarke's view, of colors, tastes, etc., is not some material substance lacking these qualities, but a mind stimulated by some material substance. So we do not yet have a clear case of something lacking a certain positive quality being the sole cause of something's having that quality.

To the second objection, Clarke replies that figure, motion, divisibility, and the like "are not real, proper, distinct and *positive powers*, but only *negative* qualities, deficiencies or imperfections. And though no cause can communicate to its effect any real perfection which it has not itself, yet the effect may easily have many imperfections, deficiencies, or negative qualities, which are not in the cause" (*Demonstration*, p. 55).

Although Clarke's response to the first objection is cogent, his response to the second is hardly adequate. The hardness of an object or its being in motion at a certain velocity do not appear to be negative qualities of the object. If being conscious is a positive quality of a certain object, it would seem that having a certain weight has as much right to the title of a positive quality.

It is understandable that Clarke should hold that the cause must have the positive qualities possessed by its effects, but need not have the limitations, deficiencies, or negative qualities of its effects. What is less clear is what possible grounds he could give for asserting that the qualities of a mind—intelligence, consciousness, etc.—are all *positive* qualities; whereas, the qualities of matter—weight, motion, figure, etc.—are all deficiencies or *negative* qualities. My suspicion is that his division of qualities into positive and negative is determined not by a consideration solely of the qualities themselves but by his religious conviction that the original cause of the universe is a purely spiritual being, lacking the primary qualities of matter. To the extent that this is his procedure, his reply to the second objection has a circular quality to it. In any case, it is clear that the principle that the cause must have whatever qualities its effects possess is meant to apply only to the *positive* qualities of the effect. And it is also clear that, holding the view that God is a purely spiritual being and also the original cause of the world, Clarke cannot but hold that the primary qualities of matter are, despite appearances to the contrary, *negative* qualities.

From all this, Clarke concludes that the only way an atheist can escape from the argument is by denying either its first or its second premise.

> There is no possibility for an atheist to avoid the force of this argument any other way, than by asserting one of these *two* things: either that there is no intelligent

being at all in the universe; or that intelligence is no distinct perfection, but merely a composition of figure and motion, as color and sounds are vulgarly supposed to be (*Demonstration*, p. 52).

Denying premise (2)—that intelligence exists in the world—is hardly possible, so the only real possibility for the atheist, on Clarke's view, is to hold the materialistic view that intelligence or intelligent activity is nothing more than a material process, "a composition of figure and motion." Against this view Clarke reasons that his opponent must either identify intelligence with particular figures and motions of matter or must hold that all matter, as matter, is somehow endowed with intelligence. The second alternative is highly implausible and probably is seriously held only by those who make subtle changes in the meaning of "intelligence." That mental activities are identical with certain physical processes, but not all, is, of course, a prominent theory that recently has gained considerable support in a form known as the Identity Theory. Clarke's reasons for rejecting such a theory are entirely *a priori*. Either the proponents of the theory simply *mean* by "intelligent activity" nothing more than these particular processes of matter; or they suppose that intelligence is a distinct quality that is possessed by matter, not itself intelligent, when that matter takes on a certain form and motion. The first alternative may be rejected for the reason that "intelligence" and "intelligent activity" do not *mean* a material process. Clarke rejects the second alternative because it is committed, he thinks, to the absurd view that the quality of intelligence is not a quality of a substance, matter, but is the quality of a quality or mode of matter. "For, in that case, not the substance itself, the particles of which the system consists, but the mere mode, the particular mode of motion and figure, would be intelligent" (*Demonstration*, p. 57). Apparently Clarke's argument is that, since intelligence is not a quality of matter as matter, it must be a quality of some quality or mode of matter. But no quality can be a quality of another quality, it can be a quality only of a substance. This objection overlooks the possibility that intelligence qualifies the *substance*, matter, but only when that matter has a particular arrangement and motion. Still it remains difficult to see how an arrangement and motion of matter should give rise to a quality—intelligence—that is fundamentally so unlike figure and motion.

It is, of course, one thing to show that the self-existent, original cause of the world is intelligent and quite another thing to show that it is *omniscient or infinitely wise*. Clarke, however, sees little difficulty in establishing the latter.

> For nothing is more evident than that an infinite, omnipresent, intelligent being must know perfectly *all things that are*; and that he who alone is self-existent and eternal, the sole cause and author of all things, from whom alone all the powers of things are derived, and on whom they continually depend, must also know perfectly all the consequences of those powers, that is, *all possibilities of things to come*, and what in every respect is best and wisest to be done (*Demonstration*, p. 109).

Apparently Clarke claims to see a necessary connection between a certain cluster of attributes—infinite, omnipresent, intelligent, eternal, and original cause of all things—and the further attribute of *infinite wisdom*. He presents little, however, in the way of argument to establish such a connection. His main argument is briefly expressed as follows:

> The supreme being because he is infinite must be everywhere present. And because he is an infinite mind or intelligence, therefore wherever he is, his knowledge is, which is inseparable from his being, and must therefore be infinite likewise (*Demonstration*, p. 109).

This argument, Clarke thinks, establishes that the self-existent being has *infinite knowledge*. But infinite knowledge must "necessarily have a full and perfect prospect of all things, and nothing can be concealed from its inspection." Consequently, the self-existent being with infinite knowledge must know whatever can be known, that is, it must be *omniscient*.

Clarke's argument, I believe, is fallacious. Let us grant that the self-existent being has been shown to be everywhere present, omnipresent, and, therefore, *infinite*. Let us also grant that the self-existent being has been shown to be intelligent and, therefore, *in some degree wise*. All that follows from this is that *whatever degree* of wisdom the self-existent being has is *everywhere present*. What does not follow is that the self-existent being has *infinite wisdom*. But it is precisely the latter conclusion that Clarke draws from his premises. I conclude, therefore, that although there may well be a necessary connection between a certain cluster of attributes—infinite, omnipresent, intelligent, etc.—and infinite wisdom, Clarke has not given a convincing argument to establish that connection.

Concerning the *power* of the self-existent being,

Clarke's sole remarks to justify his view that the self-existent being must have infinite power are the following:

> For since nothing (as has been already proved) can possibly be self-existent, besides himself, and consequently all things in the universe were made by him, and are entirely dependent upon him, and all the *powers* of all things are derived from him, and must therefore be perfectly subject and subordinate to him; it is manifest that nothing can make any difficulty or resistance to the execution of his will, but he must of necessity have absolute power to do everything he pleases, with the perfectest ease, and in the perfectest manner, at once and in a moment, whenever he wills it (*Demonstration*, p. 73).

Unfortunately nothing in these remarks seems to justify the conclusion that the self-existent being has *infinite* power. If the world derives its existence and powers from the self-existent being, the original cause of the world, then so long as the world exhibits only a finite degree of power we need suppose only that its original cause has a greater degree of power, which degree, nevertheless, may be less than infinite. If the sum of the powers in the world were infinite, Clarke's conclusion that the self-existent being has infinite power would follow. But he nowhere supposes that the finite world exhibits infinite power.

Perhaps Clarke reasons that since the self-existent being is that on which the finite world depends for its existence and powers, the self-existent being cannot have its power limited in any way by any other thing—for this other thing has whatever it has only through the self-existent being. The self-existent being, therefore, has *unlimited, infinite power.* This line of reasoning, however, is fallacious. To have infinite power is to have power that is unlimited by the powers of any other things. But the converse of this proposition need not be true. Due to the weakness of other things, a given being's power may be unlimited by the powers of other things even though its power is only finite. From the fact that nothing else has the power to prevent me from doing whatever I want to do, it does not follow that I have the power to do whatever I want to do. There may be some things I want to do but cannot do, not because some external thing has the power to prevent me, but because of the intrinsic limits of my power. To have infinite power is to have power with no extrinsic or intrinsic limits. Clarke has shown that the power of the self-existent being has no extrinsic limits. However, since he has not shown that the power of the self-existent being is intrinsically unlimited, he has failed to prove that "the self-existent being, the supreme cause of all things, must of necessity have *infinite* power."

The final feature of the theistic idea of God we shall consider is the moral attribute of *infinite goodness.* Clarke's argument to show that the self-existent, necessary being must be infinitely good or supremely perfect is complicated by the fact that it rests, in part, on a strong form of the moral theory known as *intuitionism.* According to Clarke, the basic principles of morality are objectively grounded in the nature of things and their relations of fitness and unfitness one to another. These principles, moreover, are evident to the rational intellect.

> There is therefore such a thing as fitness and unfitness, eternally, necessarily, and unchangeably in the nature

and reason of things. Now what these relations of things, absolutely and necessarily, are in themselves; that also they appear to be to the understanding of all intelligent beings, except those only who understand things to be what they are not, that is, whose understandings are either very imperfect or very much depraved (*Demonstration*, p. 115).

Clarke argues, for example, that it is *less fit or suitable* that an innocent being should be extremely and eternally miserable than that it should be free from such misery. Furthermore, that this is so is evident to any intellectual being, unless his understanding is in some way distorted. The fact that someone might deny this moral principle is, on Clarke's view, no more evidence of the subjectivity of morality than is the fact that someone fails to perceive the relation of equality between three and the square root of nine evidence that mathematical truths are not universal and necessary.

The second relevant aspect of Clarke's moral theory concerns the relation of the will to the basic principles of morality. His account approaches the view that a rational creature must act in conformity with its cognition of moral truth. If someone fails to act in conformity with morality then either his understanding is distorted so that he fails to apprehend the moral truth in question or, apprehending it, his will is swayed by self-interest, greed, etc.

And by this understanding or knowledge of the natural and necessary relations of things, *the actions likewise of all intelligent beings are constantly directed*, (which by the way is the true ground and foundation of all morality) unless their *will* be corrupted by particular interest or affection, or swayed by some unreasonable and prevailing lust (*Demonstration*, p. 115).

Presumably, then, in a being not driven by its own needs and desires, the rational apprehension of its moral duty inevitably leads it to perform its duty, if it is capable of doing so.

Given such a moral theory, I think we can see the line of reasoning by which Clarke arrives at the view that the self-existent being is morally perfect and infinitely good. For if someone fails to do what is right, there are only three accounts for that failure. He may have failed to apprehend intellectually the moral truth determining his duty, he may have apprehended the truth but his will been swayed by his own needs, lust, etc., or he may have lacked the power to perform the act in question. But none of these three accounts can apply in the case of a self-existent, omniscient, omnipotent being. Thus Clarke reasons:

The supreme cause therefore, and author of all things, since (as has already been proved) he must of necessity have infinite knowledge, and the perfection of wisdom, so that it is absolutely impossible he should err, or be in any respect ignorant of the true relations and fitness or unfitness of things, or be by any means deceived or imposed upon herein. And since he is likewise self-existent, absolutely independent and all-powerful; so that, having no want of any thing, it is impossible his will should be influenced by any wrong affection; and having no dependence, it is impossible his power should be limited by any superior strength; it is evident he must of necessity (meaning not a necessity of fate but such a moral necessity as I before said was consistent with the most perfect liberty) do always what he knows to be fittest to be done. That is, he must act always according to the strictest rules of infinite goodness, justice, and truth, and all other moral perfections (*Demonstration*, pp. 115-116).

In this chapter I have sought to give a partial account and critique of the second part of the Cosmological Argument as it is developed by its chief eighteenth-century exponent, Samuel Clarke. As we have seen, some properties of the theistic God—his eternality and infinity, for example—are shown by subtle and rather convincing arguments to belong to the self-existent, necessary being. Other properties—wisdom and power, for example—are perhaps shown to belong to the self-existent being in some finite degree. That is, given that the self-existent being is the original cause of the world and all its positive powers and perfections, Clarke's arguments to show that the self-existent being is intelligent and possessed of considerable power are plausible, if not fully persuasive. But his arguments to show that the wisdom and power of the self-existent being are *infinite* we judged to be fallacious. And in the case of one property—the infinite goodness or moral perfection—his argument was seen to rest on a rather complicated moral theory, the merit of which it is beyond the scope of this study to judge. As a general comment, however, it seems fair to say that, were the first part of the Cosmological Argument successful, the argument as a whole, while not establishing the existence of the theistic God, would provide us, nevertheless, with some rather cogent reasons for believing that there exists a deity substantially resembling, but perhaps falling short of, the God of traditional theism.

VI

The Cosmological Argument as a Justification for Belief in God

IN this study we have been concerned with explicating and evaluating the Cosmological Argument for the existence of God. In this final chapter I want to bring together our major judgments and make some final assessment of the Cosmological Argument as a possible justification for belief in God.

If the Cosmological Argument is, as its proponents contend, a *proof* of the existence of God, then it certainly provides us with a justification for the belief that God exists. But is the argument really a proof of God's existence? To answer this question fully we need to begin with a prior question: Under what conditions would an argument constitute a *proof* of the existence of God?

We need to distinguish between *proving a certain conclusion* and *constructing a proof*. By "proving a certain conclusion" I mean giving an argument for that conclusion that shows that the conclusion is true or at least probably true. To prove that God exists, in this sense, is to provide an argument that shows that it is true, or probably true, that God exists. When we ask whether God's existence can be *proved*, we are asking whether we can set forth an argument that shows that God does exist. And when we ask whether the Cosmological Argument is a *proof* of the existence of God, we

249

are asking whether it is an argument that shows that it is true that God exists.

When one *constructs a proof*, however, he need not be proving that a certain conclusion is *true*. What he may prove instead is that a certain argument is *valid* or that a certain formula is a *theorem* of the system in question. In a logic course, for example, a student may be presented with an argument and asked to construct a proof of it. If he has learned his lessons well, he will then set forth a sequence of steps, each of which is either a premise of the argument or follows from the preceding steps by one of the logical rules, and is such that the last step is the conclusion of the argument. But, of course, in constructing this proof, he has not shown that the conclusion is true, only that it logically follows from its premises. He has not, then, proved the conclusion to be true. In constructing a proof that a certain formula is a *theorem*, the student begins with the *axioms* of a certain system and by the same step-by-step procedures provides a sequence of steps, the last of which is the formula in question. Here again, however, what has been proved is not that the formula in question is *true*, only that it is deducible from certain other formulae that have been defined as the axioms of the system in question.

What we have seen thus far is that in asking whether an argument is a proof of the existence of God we are asking whether the argument shows that its conclusion is *true*, or at least *probably true*. If we return then to our question concerning the conditions an argument must satisfy in order to constitute a proof of the existence of God, it seems clear that if an argument is to be a proof of the existence of God then

> i. *the conclusion of the argument must either assert that God exists or entail (in some fairly obvious way) that God exists,*
> ii. *the conclusion must follow from the premises of the argument,*[1]

and,

> iii. *the premises of the argument must be true.*

But, just as clearly, conditions (i)–(iii) are not sufficient for an argument to be a proof of the existence of God. For consider the following argument:

> A. *1. Whatever the Bible says is true.*
> *2. The Bible says God exists.*
>
> *Therefore:*
>
> *3. God exists.*

If the premises of this argument happen to be true, the argument will satisfy conditions (i) (iii). But suppose none of us *knows* that the premises of (A) are true. In that case, (A) would not be a proof of its conclusion. For, as G. E. Moore has observed, an argument is a proof of its conclusion only if its premises are known to be

---

[1] By "follow from" I mean that the argument is either *deductively valid* or *inductively valid*. Thus the conclusion of the Cosmological Argument "follows from" its premises by virtue of the fact that it is a deductively valid argument. The Teleological Argument, however, is not deductively valid. But its conclusion may be said to "follow from" its premises by virtue of the fact that it is an inductively valid argument, its premises, if true, render it probable that the conclusion is true. Since the Cosmological Argument is the focus of our attention, in the remainder of this chapter we will be concerned with the first sense of "follow from."

true.[2] If I write down a valid argument for a conclusion
C but haven't the slightest idea as to whether its premises are true or false, then I cannot be said to have
proved that C is true—and this is so even if the premises I write down happen to be true. To say of an argument that it is a *proof* of its conclusion is to make an
epistemological as well as a logical claim about the argument; it is to imply that the premises of the argument
are known to be true. We must, then, add the condition
that (iv) the premises of the argument are known to be
true.

If we return to our basic idea that to prove that a
conclusion is true is to give an argument for that conclusion that shows that conclusion to be true, we can
perhaps see the importance of adding condition (iv).
For, we might say, an argument does not "show" the
truth of its conclusion unless it enables someone to see
or come to know that its conclusion is true. But for an
argument to enable me to come to know that its conclusion is true I must be in the position of knowing that
its premises are true. Therefore, as opposed to being
merely a *sound* argument (that is, valid with true premises) for its conclusion, an argument is a *proof* of its
conclusion only if its premises are known to be true.

Suppose that God does exist and has told me that
premise (1) in (A) is true. Suppose, that is, that the way
in which I have come to know the truth of (1) in (A) is
by knowing that God exists and that He has told me
that whatever the Bible says is true. In this case argument (A) satisfies conditions (i)–(iv). But have I in advancing (A) *proved* the existence of God?

[2] G. E. Moore, "Proof of An External World," reprinted in
G. E. Moore, *Philosophical Papers* (New York: Humanities Press,
Inc., 1959), p. 146.

In discussing *petitio principii*, Moore considers the case I have just mentioned and what he says implies that in advancing (A) I would not have proved the existence of God.

> It is natural to say:
> If S (1) knows (p) "Whatever the Bible says is true; and the Bible says God exists," and (2) *sees* that from this there follows (q) "God exists," then S has proved that God exists.
> But this is not the case.
> S will not have proved that God exists, unless *the* knowledge of p from which he inferred q was *independent* of any knowledge of q: = unless he would have had *that* knowledge of p, even if he had not known q previously, nor known previously anything else from which q followed.
> If his knowledge of p is dependent on his knowledge of (r) "The Bible was inspired by God; and whatever is said in a book inspired by God is true" then it is dependent on a previous knowledge of something else from which q follows.[3]

Moore's last remark is perhaps mistaken. The trouble with r as a basis for one's knowledge of p is not that q *follows from* r, but that one's knowledge of r appears to rest on a prior knowledge of q. If I use p to prove q, it is one thing to require that my knowledge of p not rest on or be inferred from q or from something else r which itself rests on or is inferred from q, and quite another thing to require that my knowledge of p not rest on a knowledge of anything else *from which q*

---

[3] G. E. Moore in C. Lewy, ed., *Lectures on Philosophy* (New York: Humanities Press, Inc., 1966), p. 45.

follows. Suppose I learn that (a) George Washington was a slave owner. Since I know that (b) Washington was the first U.S. President, I infer from (a) and (b) that (c) the first President of the U.S. was a slave owner. From (c) I then infer that (d) at least one U.S. President was a slave owner. On Moore's view I could not have *proved* (d) by inferring it from (c) since my knowledge of (c) was derived from the knowledge of something else— i.e., the conjunction of (a) and (b)—*from which (d) follows.*

Perhaps the point Moore was after can be put as follows: (v) in advancing an argument for C, I succeed in proving C only if my knowledge of each of the premises of the argument is not derived from my knowledge of C or from anything else which is derived from my knowledge of C.

We now have five conditions that an argument must satisfy if it is to be a *proof* of the existence of God:

i. *the conclusion asserts or entails (in some fairly obvious way) that God exists.*

ii. *the conclusion must follow from the premises of the argument.*

iii. *the premises of the argument must be true.*

iv. *the premises of the argument are known to be true.*

v. *the premises are known independently of any knowledge of the conclusion.*[4]

Before turning to the question of whether the Cosmological Argument qualifies as a proof of the existence of God, it is important to consider two differences between

---

[4] These are necessary conditions. I doubt that the list is complete. For example, it seems that an argument is a proof for me only if I *know* that its conclusion follows from its premises.

the first three and the last two conditions. Whether or not an argument satisfies the first three conditions is quite independent of what any human being (or any conscious being) knows or thinks. For example, that the conclusion of an argument logically follows from the argument's premises is a matter that is completely unaffected by what anyone knows or thinks. It is obvious, however, that whether an argument satisfies conditions (iv) and (v) is not independent of what anyone knows or thinks.

A second difference is that we can intelligently ask "by whom?" concerning conditions (iv) and (v), but cannot raise this question concerning conditions (i), (ii), and (iii). The premises of an argument may be known by Smith and not known by Jones; and the premises may be known independently of the conclusion by Smith but not be known independently of the conclusion by Brown. Conditions (iv) and (v), then, are *person-relative* in two ways. First, neither condition can hold independently of what some person knows or thinks. Second, once we ask the question "by whom?" it is natural to think of conditions (iv) and (v) holding for one person but not for another.

Consider condition (iv). Since the premises of an argument may be known by Smith and not by Brown, how strong should we make condition (iv)? Shall we say that an argument is a proof of its conclusion only if its premises are known *by every human being*? Clearly not. For it is doubtful that any argument is such that its premises are known by absolutely everyone. I suggest that we understand (iv) as: the premises of the argument are known to be true *by some human being*. Of course, if we follow this convention it would be possible for someone to write down an argument that is a *proof* of its conclusion even if *he* does not know that the premises of the argument are true—for all we are requiring is that *some* human being know that its premises are true. Similarly, if we follow this procedure for condition (v), I may write down an argument that is a *proof* of its conclusion even though my knowledge of the premises is dependent on my knowledge of the conclusion—for all we are requiring is that some human being's knowledge of the premises is independent of whatever knowledge he has of the conclusion.

The above notion of "proof" corresponds to the first way in which (iv) and (v) are person-relative. It is important, I think, to have a second notion of "proof" corresponding to the second way in which (iv) and (v) are person-relative. An argument, I shall say, is a *proof for x* only if its premises are *known by x* and *x*'s knowledge of the premises is independent of any knowledge x has of the conclusion of the argument. Since you may know some propositions to be true that I do not, an argument in which those propositions figure as premises may be a proof for you and not a proof for me.

If we bring together the two notions of "proof," it should be clear that an argument I am considering may be, at one and the same time, a proof of its conclusion and not a proof for me of its conclusion. This will be so just in case there is some human being (other than myself) for whom it is a proof. An argument is a proof of its conclusion if and only if there is some human being such that the argument in question is a *proof for that person*.

The distinction between *being a proof* (i.e., being a proof for some human being) and *being a proof for me* is relevant to our assessment of the worth of an argument. I may have two arguments for a given conclusion C, both of which are *proofs for me*. The premises of one of the arguments, however, may be such that only I, or very few people, know them to be true; whereas, the premises of the other argument may be such that many people either do know them or, in contrast to the premises of the first argument, can easily come to know them. If my purpose is not to present just a proof of C, but a proof of C that will enable others to come to know that C, it is clear that the second argument is superior to the first. (Some theists may regard the Cosmological Argument as superior to the Ontological Argument for just this reason.)

Is the Cosmological Argument a *proof* of the existence of God? As we have just seen, to ask this question is not to ask whether the argument is a proof for me, but whether the argument is a *proof for anyone*. On this question, it seems to me that the critics of natural theology are right—the Cosmological Argument is not a proof of the existence of God. My agreement with the critics, however, does not run very deep. For, as I have argued in this study, most of the *reasons* that the modern-day critics of the Cosmological Argument— Russell, Edwards, Flew, Smart, Hepburn, etc.—give in support of their critical assessment of the argument do not justify that critical assessment. What, then, are the reasons that have been given in support of the view that the Cosmological Argument is not a *proof* of the existence of God?

As we noted at the outset of this study, the Cosmological Argument has two distinct parts. The first part purports to establish that there exists a logically necessary being, and the second part purports to establish that the necessary being (whose existence has been established) is God.[5] Since our study has focused primarily on the first part of the argument, and since the major philosophical objections have been directed against this part, I shall confine this review of the major criticisms to those directed against that part of the argument that purports to establish that there exists a logically necessary being.

Is the following argument (i.e., Part I of the Cosmological Argument) a proof of its conclusion?

1. *Every being is either a dependent being or an independent being.*
2. *Not every being is a dependent being.*

Therefore:

3. *There exists an independent being.*

Therefore:

4. *There exists a necessary being.*

We have examined a number of objections to this argument and to the reasoning its proponents give in support of its premises, objections such that, if they are correct, it follows that the argument is not a proof of its conclusion. Indeed, if some of the objections advanced by modern-day critics of the argument are cor-

---

[5] By "the Cosmological Argument" I refer here to what we have seen to be its most significant version, the 18th-century version set forth by Samuel Clarke. Since our study of that argument has been spread over several chapters, it is useful to bring together here the major criticisms of it which have been discussed in those several chapters. The major criticisms of the historically significant 13th-century verisons of the argument are to be found in Chapter I.

rect, the premises of the argument are false or, if not false, based on fallacious reasoning. The major objections we have examined may be summarized as follows:

1. *The first premise of the argument is false or, at least not known to be true.*

2. *The reasoning given in support of the second premise*
   a. *is fallacious since it applies to the collection of dependent beings a property which is applicable only to the members of the collection.*
   b. *is fallacious because it infers that the collection of dependent beings has a property from the premise that each of its members has that property.*
   c. *is fallacious because it assumes that to require an explanation of the existence of the collection of dependent beings is to require something over and above an explanation of the existence of each of the members of the collection.*

3. *The conclusion of the argument is false since it is impossible for there to exist a logically necessary being.*
   a. *logical necessity applies to propositions, not things.*
   b. *necessary propositions are assertions that one concept stands in a certain relation to another concept, but existence is not a concept or characteristic; hence, an existential proposition is not an assertion of a relation between concepts and, hence, cannot be necessarily true.*

c. *necessary propositions merely reflect our use of words and, therefore, provide us no information about the world; but existential propositions depend for their truth on what objects the world contains and, therefore, cannot be necessarily true.*

The first premise of the Cosmological Argument expresses one form of the Principle of Sufficient Reason. The premise implies that for every existing being there is an explanation of why that being exists. The explanation for a given being's existence, the premise asserts, is to be found either within other beings and their causal activities or within the being's own nature. Some critics (e.g., A. Flew) argue that the premise is false on the grounds that every explanatory sequence must stop with something that is left unexplained, a brute fact as it were. But this point is simply a statement about our limitations—we cannot explain everything and, therefore, must stop with something that we use to explain other things but is itself left unexplained. The objection does not show that there is something *in nature* for which there is or can be no explanation. Flew claims that his criticism is not simply a statement about our limitations, but is derived from the very concept of explanation. But if the concept of explanation itself requires that not everything can have an explanation, this must be shown by an *analysis* of the concept of explanation. It is insufficient simply to cite, as Flew does, a few examples of explanations in which something is left unexplained. The claim, then, that the Cosmological Argument is unsound because its first premise is false is a claim that—if we take Flew's argument as typical— is poorly argued for in the literature.

It will be recalled that I presented an argument designed to show that an important version of the Principle of Sufficient Reason (PSR) is false. But the form of PSR that I sought to prove false is a good deal stronger than the form of the principle that constitutes the first premise of the Cosmological Argument. The strongest form of PSR is

> *PSR1: Every actual state of affairs has a reason either within itself or in some other state of affairs.*

Whereas, the form of PSR constituting premise one is:

> *PSR2: Every existing thing has a reason for its existence either in the necessity of its own nature or in the causal efficacy of some other beings.*

I sought to establish that PSR1 is false. But even here it must be admitted that my argument rested on an unproven—although I think reasonable—assumption: namely, that it is a contingent fact that any contingent being exist. My argument, however, is simply inapplicable to PSR2. And, as I have indicated, no one has put forth any convincing argument for the falsity of PSR2.

It is, of course, one thing to claim that the first premise (PSR2) of the Cosmological Argument is false and quite another thing to claim that no human being knows that it is true. It is the latter claim I have supported in this study and which, it seems to me, has sufficient support to warrant the conclusion that the Cosmological Argument is not a proof of the existence of God. For when we examine what the supporters of PSR2 say in its behalf, it becomes reasonably clear that none of them has knowledge of the truth of PSR2. Some hold that PSR2 is known because it is proved from other things we know. But an examination of the main arguments that supposedly demonstrate PSR2 showed them to be notoriously bad and, therefore, incapable of enabling anyone to come to know the truth of PSR2. Some hold that PSR2 is known intuitively, that it is a self-evident truth as clear to reason as that two plus two equals four. Against this view, I argued that PSR2 is neither analytically true nor a synthetic necessary truth, known *a priori*, and, hence, is not a self-evident truth known intuitively. Finally, we noted that some recent supporters of PSR2 take the view that it is neither a self-evident truth nor demonstrable by reason. Instead they argue that PSR2 is a fundamental presupposition of reason, something which, as Taylor puts it, "all men, whether they ever reflect upon it or not, seem more or less to presuppose." Concerning this view, I noted first that from the fact that I may presuppose the truth of some proposition p it does not follow that I know that p is true—nor does it follow that p is true. Nature is not bound to satisfy our presuppositions. Hence, the presupposition view of PSR2 does not support the claim that the Cosmological Argument is a proof of its conclusion. Indeed, that we presuppose PSR2 is consistent with the first premise of the Cosmological Argument (i.e., PSR2) being false.

Second, I raised the question whether it is indeed true that all men presuppose PSR2. We must be careful to distinguish the principle

A. *Whatever begins to exist must have an explanation of its existence.*

from the stronger principle

B. *Whatever exists (even if it has always existed)
   must have an explanation of its existence.*

A, I suggested, may well be a presupposition of the
common-sense view of the world. But it is not clear that
B is such a presupposition. And it is B, i.e., PSR2, that
is asserted by the first premise of the Cosmological
Argument.

Finally, I noted that although the view that PSR2 is
a presupposition does not show that the Cosmological
Argument is a proof—or even that it is a sound argument—it does have an interesting implication for our
assessment of the argument. For if Taylor and Copleston are correct, then if we reject the Cosmological Argument we must, on pain of inconsistency, reject it on
grounds other than its appeal to PSR2. If to presuppose PSR2 is, among other things, to believe that
PSR2 is true, then we cannot reject the Cosmological
Argument solely because of its appeal in its first premise to PSR2.

Concerning the three objections to the reasoning by
which the proponent of the argument endeavors to support the second premise, I argued that each of the objections fails to show that the reasoning is fallacious. The
first objection is that the reasoning is fallacious because
it applies to the collection of dependent beings a property (having a cause or explanation) that is applicable
only to the members of the collection. In examining
this objection, I distinguished various senses that might
be given to the question "Why does the collection of
dependent beings exist?" I argued (i) that the question
does make sense when viewed as a request for an explanation of why there are any dependent beings at all,

and (ii) that it was this view that the proponents had in mind when they argued that the collection itself requires a cause or explanation.

The second objection charges that the reasoning in support of the second premise commits the fallacy of composition, the fallacy of inferring that the collection of dependent beings has a certain property (having an explanation) from the premise that each of the members of the collection has that property. This objection, I argued, is simply inapplicable to the reasoning of some of the major proponents of the argument. Samuel Clarke, for example, appeals to the Principle of Sufficient Reason as the basis for the claim that the collection of dependent beings must itself have an explanation of its existence. He simply does not make the inference that the objection alleges is made.

The final objection against the reasoning in support of the second premise is that it assumes that to explain the existence of the collection is something over and above explaining the existence of the members of the collection. As Hume, who first advanced the objection, remarked, "Did I show you the particular causes of each individual in a collection of twenty particles of matter, I should think it very unreasonable, should you afterwards ask me, what was the cause of the whole twenty. This is sufficiently explained in explaining the cause of the parts." In response to this objection, I argued that when the existence of each member of a collection is explained by reference to some other member *of that very same collection* then it does not follow that the collection itself has an explanation. For it is one thing for there to be an explanation of the existence of each dependent being and quite another thing for there to be an explanation of why there are dependent beings at all. And when the explanation for each dependent being is the causal activity of some other dependent being *ad infinitum* it will be true that there is an explanation for each dependent being but false that there is an explanation for why there are any dependent beings at all.

The final set of objections we have considered in this study are directed at the conclusion of Part I of the Cosmological Argument. They purport to *establish* that the conclusion "There exists a (logically) necessary being" is false. The first objection, "logical necessity applies to propositions, not things," at best shows only that when we say of some being *x* that it is a logically necessary being, what we say must be explicated in terms of some *proposition* asserting the existence of *x* being logically necessary. The intent of the objection is not to show directly that there cannot be a logically necessary being, but to show that *x* is a logically necessary being only if some proposition asserting the existence of *x* is necessarily true. I argued in support of this point.

The two major objections to the conclusion of the Cosmological Argument depend on an acceptance of the point just made. For they, if successful, show only that no existential proposition is necessarily true. In response to each of these objections I argued that it rested on unestablished claims about necessarily true propositions. The first objection rests on the principle that a proposition is necessary only if it asserts that concepts are related in a certain manner; the second rests on the principle, associated with the conventionalist's theory of truth, that a necessarily true proposition (i) is necessarily true solely because of the rules governing our use of symbols, and (ii) conveys no information concerning the constituents of the real world. Neither of these principles, I argued, is sufficiently established to enable us to know that no existential proposition can be a necessary truth. Hence, while conceding that the objections to the conclusion may provide us with some reasonable doubts concerning the existence of a logically necessary being, I argued that they are not of sufficient strength to refute in advance any argument that purports to establish the existence of such a being. These objections against the idea of a necessary being, I suggested, must be weighed in the balance with whatever rational grounds the Cosmological Argument provides us for thinking that there does exist a logically necessary being.

It is apparent from our review of the major objections to the Cosmological Argument that the critics of the argument view their criticisms as establishing that the Cosmological Argument not only fails as a *proof* of the existence of God but also can be seen to contain false premises, premises arrived at by fallacious reasoning, and a false conclusion. That is, the thrust of the major objections we have considered is to *establish* that the Cosmological Argument is *unsound*. So viewed, the conclusion of this study is that the criticisms are a *failure*. On the other hand, we have also concluded that the argument cannot pass muster as a proof of the existence of God. For each of its premises has been shown either to express or to rest on an unknown—if not unknowable—principle, the Principle of Sufficient Reason. Perhaps the truth we can *know* about the Cosmological Argument is this. Although it may be a perfectly sound argument, it cannot reasonably be maintained to be a proof of its conclusion. For although its premises may be true, we are not in the position of knowing that they are true. And since to claim of an argument that it is a

266

proof of its conclusion is to imply that its premises are known to be true, we are not entitled to claim that the Cosmological Argument is a proof of the existence of a necessary being.

I am aware that this modest conclusion will satisfy neither the proponents of the argument nor its critics. The critics wish to show that the argument is invalid, contains false premises, or premises arrived at by fallacious reasoning. And if our judgment is correct, this wish must go unfulfilled. The proponents wish to show that the argument provides a good and conclusive reason for accepting its conclusion. This wish, too, must remain unfulfilled. Like most important philosophical arguments, it appears that the Cosmological Argument is neither as good as its supporters have claimed nor as bad as its critics have believed.

In bringing this study to a close I want to suggest that the Cosmological Argument, despite its failure to be a proof of the existence of God, may yet have some epistemological value for theism. For if we examine the arguments by which we shape our beliefs, the sad fact is that only a few of them qualify as *proofs* of their conclusions, only a few of them enable us to *know* that their conclusions are true or probably true. There are many deductively valid arguments whose premises we have reasons to believe, thus making it reasonable for us to accept their conclusions, even though none of us can claim to *know* that the premises of these arguments, or their conclusions, are true. Perhaps, then, the Cosmological Argument makes theistic belief reasonable, even though it fails as a proof of theistic belief.

Let us say that an argument is an acceptable argument for its conclusion only if *i. its conclusion follows from its premises,*

and,

ii. it is reasonable for someone to believe that its premises are true.[6]

If these conditions prevail, it may be reasonable for someone to accept the conclusion of such an argument, that is, reasonable for him to believe that the conclusion is true, even though he does not *know* that the conclusion is true. (It is often reasonable for us to believe things to be true that we do not know to be true—as any weatherman will testify.) Our question, then, is whether the Cosmological Argument is an *acceptable* argument for its conclusion.

Because the premises of the Cosmological Argument rest on a principle—the Principle of Sufficient Reason—that appears to be unknowable, I concluded that the Cosmological Argument is not only not a proof for me, it is not a proof for anyone. But if we turn to the question of whether it is reasonable for me or for anyone else to believe the Principle of Sufficient Reason, it is less than clear that our answer should be *negative*. Possibly, then, the theist is entitled to claim that the Cosmological Argument is an acceptable argument for theistic belief, that it shows the reasonableness of belief in God, even though it does not demonstrate the existence of God.[7]

[6] These are necessary, and the most important, conditions an argument must satisfy to be an acceptable argument for its conclusion. They are not, however, sufficient. Also, it should be noted that an acceptable argument for a conclusion need not have *true* premises—for it is often reasonable to believe something to be true which, in fact, is false.

[7] It is necessary to point out, however, that our study of the

A Justification for Belief in God

I do not propose here to endorse the view that the Cosmological Argument is an acceptable argument for its conclusion. I am proposing to the theist that in seeking rational justification for his belief in the conclusion of the Cosmological Argument he would do well to abandon the view that the Cosmological Argument is a proof of theism, and, in its place, pursue the possibility that the Cosmological Argument shows the reasonableness of theistic belief, even though it perhaps fails to show that theism is true.

---

second part of the Cosmological Argument shows that at best that part of the argument proves, or makes it reasonable to believe, that a self-existent being would have some of the features the theistic God has in an infinite degree, but fails to show or make it reasonable to believe that the self-existent being has these features in an *infinite* degree.

Index

Adams, Robert M., 216n
analytically false, 80
analytically true, 79
Anselm, St., 52, 224
a posteriori, 83
a priori, 83
Aquinas, St. Thomas, 68n, 121,
173; assumptions at work in
the first two ways, 38; fallacy
in the third way, 42-43; first
way, 10-19; on an infinite
regress of causes, 22-23; on
necessary being, 40-41; second way, 19-38; third way,
39-45
argument, acceptable, 267-68;
A posteriori and *a priori*, 3
Ayer, A. J., 219

Bettoni, Efrem, 51n
Bonaventure, St., 121
Boole, George, 8
Brown, Patterson, 26n, 40n,
41n, 203n
brute facts, Aquinas's re-
jection of, 17
Butler, Joseph, criticism of
Clarke on infinity, 229ff

causal series, accidentally ordered and per se ordered,
23-29

cause, temporally prior and
causally prior, 30
change, an infinite regress of
changes, 18-19; Aquinas's
view of, 12; nothing can
change itself, 13-18
Chisholm, Roderick, 82n
Clarke, Samuel, 8, 55-58, 61,
67-68, 83-84, 99, 112n, 117,
120-21, 160, 181-93, 192, 224-
25, 227-28, 238, 239, 242-43;
on eternal yet caused, 68 69;
on whether something has
always existed, 61-70; recon-
struction of his argument for
a necessary being, 168-69;
response to Butler on infinity, 230ff
collection, concrete and abstract, 134-35
contingent, 82
conventionalism, 218-19; theory
of necessary truth, 220
Copleston, F. C., 11n, 30, 43,
86, 88, 129

de dicto, 173-75
dependent being, argument
against an infinite succession
of, 120-21; assumption that
an infinite succession of must
be explained, 123-24; de-

271

Index

*Library of Congress Cataloging
in Publication Data*

Rowe, William L
    The cosmological argument.

    Includes bibliographical references.
    1. God—Proof, Cosmological. I. Title.
BT102.R69   231'.042   74-25628
ISBN 0-691-07210-8